AF333539

Willmore Horseback Adventure

Adventures
With
Grandchildren

OTHER BOOKS BY ALLEN JOHNSON

Drive Through Russia? Impossible – 1986

**Canoeing the Wabash
Adventures with Grandchildren – 1991**

**Biking Across the Devil's Backbone
Adventures with Grandchildren – 1997**

**Australia from the Back of a Camel
Adventures with Grandchildren – 1999**

**Biking to the Arctic Circle
Adventures with Grandchildren – 2000**

Genealogy of the Johnson Family – 2001

**Rollerblading Across Holland
Adventures with Grandchildren – 2002**

**Kayaking Around Iceland
Adventures with Grandchildren – 2003**

Willmore Horseback Adventure

Adventures
With
Grandchildren

Allen L. Johnson

Creative Enterprises

Dayton, Ohio

PHOTO CREDIT

Page 8 . . . . **Willis Anderson**
Page 81 . . . . **Anna Carnell**
Page 7 . . . . **Bill Chugahnman**
Page 17, 79, 97, 105, 108, 114, 119, 122, 132 **Mark Lund**
Pages 61 . . . . **Ray Rasmussen**
Pages 23, 24, 32, 37, 51, 53, 54, 59, 60, 73, 76, 82, 87, 88, 91, 94, 99, 104, 110, 116, 117, 129, 130, 135, 142, 143, 146, 150, 152, 155, 156 . . . . **Florence Ross**
Page 77, 90. **Lee Snipes**
Page 46 . . . . **Don Streubel**
Page 49 . . . . **Brian Wolitski**
All other photos . . . . **Author**

FIRST EDITION

All Rights reserved, including the right of reproduction in whole or in part in any form.

Copyright © 2004 by Allen L. Johnson

Published by Creative Enterprises
1040 Harvard Blvd; Dayton OH 45406-5047

Printed by Sheridan Books Inc
Ann Arbor, Michigan

Manufactured in the United States of America
ISBN: 1-880675-08-0

DEDICATION

This book is dedicated to the Wild Rose Outfitters who took excellent care of us on the ride and to our hiking companions who offered us friendship, advise and allowed me to publish their outstanding photographs. The author also wants to thank the following people for their editorial and proofreading assistance:

Wendy Bush
Anna and Dave Carnell
Margaret Cotton
Gloria Johnson – chief editor and consultant
Mark and Lois Lund
Dave Manzer
Marilyn Manzer
Florence Ross
Linda Schwartz

CONTENTS

ILLUSTRATIONS

Willmore Horseback Adventure

Adventures
With
Grandchildren

Chapter 1

The Adventure Plan

"Can we go horseback riding this weekend?" Emily asked every weekend from March through May.

"Can we trot?" Jessica asked the ride leader as our horses walked the trails through Englewood Park.

"How come we can't ride longer, Grandpa?" Emily complained after our one-hour trail ride.

"How about a horseback adventure this summer where you can ride all day and trot all you want?" I asked my 9-year-old twin granddaughters.

"Yeahhhhhhhhhhhhhh!" Emily and Jessica agreed.

That's how the Great Willmore Horseback Adventure came to be. Originally I considered taking the girls on a two-week-long wagon train ride up the Oregon Trail. While searching the Internet for a honest-to-goodness old-time wagon train ride through the desert, I located a four-day ride in a rubber-tired wagon along the back roads of Wyoming and a three-day trip through the grasslands of Colorado, but no long, desert rides. Next I expanded the search to include a long horseback ride along rugged mountain trails. I found an company called "Wild Rose Outfitters" that offered various length ride over "Some of the most beautiful trails in the Canadian Rocky Mountains." I called Dave Manzer, the head of Wild Rose and explained I'd like to take my 9-year-old granddaughters on a two-week horseback ride.

"We have a 16-day trail ride in Willmore Wilderness Park that the girls could probably accomplish," Dave said.

"Could you e-mail me a description of the Willmore ride?" I asked.

"I'll send it to you right now," Dave promised.

"Journey with us into the heart of Willmore Wilderness Park, a place some call Riding-in-the-Sky Country," the e-mailed brochure read. "We travel on historic trails made by native people, explorers, trappers and hunters. Alberta's Willmore Wilderness Park is true Rocky Mountain wilderness without roads, buildings or bridges. We'll visit remote lakes, enjoy the wild flowers, and scout for big horn sheep, mountain goats, elk, caribou, moose, mule deer, grizzly bears, black bears and mountain lions."

I discussed the planned trip with my daughter, Judy, and granddaughters. They agreed to the July dates. My wife, Gloria, would be in Wisconsin at her annual knitting camp while we were gone so those dates wouldn't interfere with any family plans.

"I'd like to sign Emily and Jessica up for horse camp to improve their riding skills before we take the trip," I told Judy and the twins. The Englewood Riding Stables runs weeklong horse camps during the summer to familiarize youngsters with the care of horses, horse safety and riding skills.

"Okay," everyone agreed.

In early June Emily and Jessica spent a week at horse camp. For five-hours-a-day they learned how to clean their horses, brush them, clean their hooves with a hoof pick and brush, put the bridle and saddle on and ride. They enjoyed cleaning out the stalls because they could be near the horses. During the week, they learned the names of the different parts of the horses and the names of the different genders and ages of horses. Emily became proficient in trotting on Tory and Jessica on Tristan. They even learned to canter. The trainers divided the trainees into two teams and kept track during the week of each team's scores on getting their chores done on time, courtesy, skill and attention to the task at hand. Emily and Jessica's team won the weeklong competition and got to choose their prize. They chose to ride bareback.

"Could both teams ride bareback?" Emily asked the lady in charge.

"That's a very good idea," she agreed, so they shared their prize with the losing team.

On the last day, the camp held a parade to show what the kids had learned. Our granddaughters spent all morning brushing their horses and decorating them with ribbons, buntings, beads and braids. They all looked great as they rode around the ring and made us very proud of their accomplishments.

In the meantime, I finalized the trail ride agreement, made airline reservations to Edmonton, Alberta, reserved a rental car to get us to the trail head and decided what we should take on the trip. The ride instructions recommended warm clothes since we would be riding in the mountains above the tree line. I made out lists for myself and my granddaughters (Appendix A).

Judy and I signed the Recreational Activity Release and Indemnity Agreement, promising not to sue Wild Rose if we got injured on the trip. Reading the agreement almost makes a person want to go back to bed and cover his head.

"Horses may, at any time, without warning, and for no reason, jump up, forward, backwards or sideways.

Horses may become uncontrollable, run wildly, buck, kick, rear up, or step on feet or other body parts without warning.

Horses may trip, stumble and/or fall down when being led, ridden or otherwise attended.

Horses may become tired, stressed, cantankerous and their behavior is unpredictable.

The signer understands that these risks, and others, are inherent with horses and other activities where risks may not be anticipated, controlled, or eliminated by the Provider, and further, the Provider has no duty to do so."

I ordered thirty topographic maps covering the Willmore Wilderness area and started reading up on the Canadian Rocky Mountains to get an idea of what to expect on the ride. I anticipated that riding eight-hours-a-day with my granddaughters and camping out at freezing temperatures would be an adventure. Author Louis L'amour defines *adventure* as a romantic name for *trouble*.

"What people speak of as adventure," Louis writes, "is something nobody in his right mind would seek out, and it becomes romantic only when one is safely at home!"

Bring on the adventure!

Chapter 2

Where is Rock Lake Lodge?

"We have to get up at what time?" Jessica asked when I told them we were leaving early for the airport.

"Four in the morning," I said.

"It's not even light then," Emily said.

I checked Emily's and Jessica's luggage to make sure they had their boots, long underwear, hats, coats and gloves. The girls packed their things in individual soft camp bags and then those bags went into heavy canvas duffel bags that could be packed on the horses. Next I went over my list to make sure I had the sleeping bags, air mattresses, a compass and maps.

Since we had to leave so early, Emily and Jessica slept over at our house. About 8 o'clock Sunday night I suggested the girls take their baths and get ready for bed. They had all their clothes packed so I washed what they were wearing while they took their baths. Then I dried their underwear with a hair dryer so they would have something to wear to bed. Gloria provided the girls with long T-shirts to wear as nighties. Their jeans and shirts could dry overnight in the dryer and would be ready for them in the morning.

Gloria helped me load the girls and 150 pounds of luggage into the car at 5 a.m. Emily and Jessica slept most of the way to the airport. We checked in at Northwest Airlines and then went to the snack bar and ordered a glass of milk and a chocolate muffin for breakfast. Emily and Jessica played with a blue-eyed baby sitting next to us while waiting for our flight. A little before 9 a.m. we boarded the two-engine jet and found our seats. Emily sat by the window for the first flight and Jessica got the window seat for the second flight. Once airborne we played Kings-in-the-Corners, read the first part of "Changes for Kaya" (the story of an Indian girl and her horse) and wrote letters to their mother. About 1 p.m. the plane landed in Edmonton, Alberta, Canada. While passing through customs and immigration we had to show our passports and I had to produce a letter signed by Judy showing permission to travel with my granddaughters. Apparently child kidnapping by relatives is a problem.

We rented a Toyota Echo from Thrifty and headed out of Edmonton. The only time I had been to Edmonton was in 1999 when I rode my bicycle through on the way to Alaska. It took us an hour to get from the airport on the south side of Edmonton, through downtown to the west side of the city. Once out of the city we stopped at Tim Hortons in Spruce Grove for supper. I bought Canadian postage stamps and mailed the letters Emily and Jessica wrote to their mother. We would not have access to a mailbox on the horseback ride.

We took the Yellowhead Highway three hours west and stopped at the Dairy Queen in Hinton for ice cream. There would be no ice cream in the backcountry for the next 16 days.

"One hot fudge sundae with chocolate ice cream and two hot fudge sundaes with regular ice cream," I told the waitress.

"We don't have chocolate ice cream," the waitress said.

"No chocolate!" Emily moaned. "Canada is just like Iceland." (We couldn't get chocolate ice cream in Iceland during our 2002 trip there). Emily only likes chocolate ice cream. She ended up ordering a chocolate-covered Dilly Bar and eating the chocolate coating before giving me the vanilla ice cream.

I drove up Route 40 toward Grande Cache and turned off at the Rock Lake Lodge sign.

"There's a moose!" Emily shouted as we started down the gravel road. A huge moose looked up from the meadow and watched us as we drove slowly by.

"You watch out the left side for animals, Jessica, I'll watch out the right side and Grandpa can watch out the front," Emily suggested.

Emily spotted a moose as we turned off the highway

"Horses up ahead," I said as we rounded a corner and came upon six beautiful horses standing in the middle of the road.

"They're wearing bells and have something around their front feet," Jessica pointed out.

"Those are hobbles to keep them from straying too far from home and the bells help locate them," I said. "See how they hop when they try to run." They hopped along like rocking horses as they moved off the road into the forest.

"There's some deer," Jessica yelled as thirty elk walked out of the forest and meandered across the road. I stopped the car; the elk didn't seem concerned. The herd walked slowly across the road and stopped to graze on the tender grass along the side. The bucks had huge racks that extended three or four feet above their heads. Majestically they threw their heads back so their antlers

A bull elk walked out of the forest to graze beside the road

wouldn't catch on the branches as they sauntered off into the forest. We sat there until the last fawn melted into the dark forest.

About forty-five minutes down the gravel road I came to a sign for Rock Lake Lodge. I turned into the woods and passed a nice house before coming to a stop by half-a-dozen log cabins. There was no sign to indicate whether the house was the lodge. The road ended at the cabins so I parked the car and walked up to the front porch of the house. A huge brown Labrador Retriever stood on the porch and barked.

"Nice doggie," I said as I eased up the steps with my hand out, palm up. The dog smelled my hand and decided to let me pass. I knocked on the door and a lady answered.

"Hi. I'm Allen Johnson here with my granddaughters. Is this Rock Lake Lodge?"

"Yes," the lady said showing no sign of recognition.

"We have a reservation here tonight," I said, showing her the paper from Wild Rose.

Jessica and Emily sat on the log and threw rocks

"We weren't expecting anyone," the lady said, "but we have one cabin left. Sally will take you down there."

Sally led us back to the cabin and unlocked the front door.

"I'm sorry about the dead flies on the floor," she said as she showed us around the one-room cabin.

"That's okay," I said. "We'll sweep those up. What time is breakfast?"

"About 8 o'clock, if that's okay," Sally said. "Dave doesn't usually get here before 9 o'clock to pick you up. There's wood on the porch for the stove," Sally said as she left.

The cabin had no electricity and no gas, but it did have cold running water, a sink, a toilet, a wood stove and two double beds.

Emily, Jessica and I walked through the woods to the creek. The girls played on a nine-inch diameter log that spanned the creek. First they crossed the creek back and forth on the log and then they sat in the middle and threw stones in the water. The mosquitoes were pretty bad so we put on bug repellent. After an hour of playing by the creek, we walked back to the cabin and I started a fire in the wood stove. I heated some water and made hot chocolate for us.

"There's a big spider in the bathroom," Jessica yelled.

I found the broom and dispatched the spider.

Emily started sweeping the dead flies, sticks and leaves out of the cabin. Jessica found another spider under the bed. She was my chief spider finder and Emily was my chief sweeper. The sun still shown through the window when we went to bed around 10:30 p.m. Mountain Time (12:30 a.m. Dayton time). The cabin was warm and quiet—great sleeping.

I woke up to the sound of horses whinnying. Looking out the window, I saw half a dozen horses in the meadow next to the cabin. I started a fire in the stove and put the kettle on for tea. When I washed my hands, the water was so cold it hurt. There was frost on the porch. Welcome to the mountains.

Emily and Jessica woke up about 7 o'clock and dressed by the warm stove. An hour later we walked up to the lodge and Donna, the owner's wife, made us pancakes, bacon and eggs for breakfast. As we ate, the owner, George Kelley came in and sat down.

"My great-grandfather settled this area about a hundred years ago," George told us. "I built this lodge and the cabins. I hunt, fish, trap and work as a guide while my wife and sister-in-law run the lodge."

"When I was a boy, I used to trap," I said. "I had big plans of moving to British Columbia after high school and trapping marten for a living. Do you trap marten here?"

"Oh, yeah," George said with a smile. "One year I caught 120, but then the bottom dropped out of the fur market so I quit. The price is back up now and I average about 50 marten a year."

"Do you have wolverines around here?" I asked. "I understand they can mess up your trap line and are difficult to catch."

"Yeah, a wolverine will steal the martens out of the traps, but they're not difficult to catch. I just set a snare on a pole with some bait on the end and the wolverine will go for it every time," George said as he drew me a sketch of his wolverine snare setup. "What did you trap?"

"I used to trap muskrats in the farm ditches in Illinois when I was in high school," I said.

"My mother stepped in a muskrat hole in the dark and a muskrat bit her on the leg," Donna said. "It was a nasty bite and took a long time to heal. I've been afraid of muskrats ever since."

"The fishers (a large dark brown arboreal carnivorous mammal related to the weasels) are the animal you have to watch out for," George said. "They are bad tempered and vicious. One time my partner and I caught a fisher in our trap and I hit it on the head to kill it. I threw that fisher in the back of my panel truck and started down the road to my next trap. Well now, that fisher came to and started running around inside the truck and growling as I drove down the road. My partner grabbed his rifle and pointed it at the fisher.

"Don't shoot in here," I yelled.

'I'm not going to shoot,' he said, 'I just want it to bite down on the barrel so I can club him.'

"We finally knocked that fisher out and killed him with a knife. A mad fisher is nothing to mess with," George concluded.

Chapter 3

Eagle's Nest Camp

A bull elk walked into the meadow by Rock Lake Lodge and started grazing along with George's horses.

"Aren't the elk afraid of people?" I asked.

"Only during hunting season," George replied.

Dave Manzer, the fifty-four-year-old Wild Rose outfitter who would be our guide, came in, introduced himself and sat down at the breakfast table. Donna poured him a cup of coffee.

"We're up at the trail head loading the packhorses," Dave said. "Are you guys about ready to head out?"

"Yeah," I said. "We're all packed up. Give us a minute to grab our stuff and we'll be ready to go." Emily, Jessica and I walked back to the cabin, brushed our teeth, threw our gear in the car and drove back to the lodge. Dave came out and we followed his truck up the gravel road to Rock Lake Staging Area. The staging area consisted of a big gravel parking lot, several corrals, a watering trough, a small trailer and two toilets.

Emily and Jessica immediately went over to one of the corrals and started petting the horses. There were a lot more horses in the corral than I expected.

"How many horses are you taking?" I asked Dave.

"We'll have 10 riding horses and 24 packhorses," Dave said.

"Why so many packhorses?"

"We'll be carrying about two tons of food and equipment and each horse can only carry about a 160-pound pack."

"What in the world are you packing that weighs two tons?" I asked.

"Well," Dave replied as he rubbed his beard and looked up as though he expected Divine help, "we've got frozen steaks, fresh fruit, canned goods, tents, sleeping bags, a camp stove, a complete blacksmith shop, chain saws, axes, shovels, horse food, my guitar and Anna's fiddle."

While the wranglers loaded stuff in huge plastic pack-boxes, I went over to meet the other travelers.

"Hi, I'm Mark Lund and this is my wife, Lois," a middle-aged man with a salt and pepper beard said as he grabbed my hand with a firm grip.

"I'm Allen Johnson and those are my granddaughters, Emily and Jessica," I replied as I shook hands and pointed out the girls by the corral. "Are you hikers?"

"Yeah. We may ride a little when you explore some of the mountain passes. This is our dog, Gimli," Mark said as he pointed to a 50-pound, male Airedale that smelled my leg. "He's harmless."

"Hi. I'm Florence Ross, another one of the hikers," an attractive lady wearing a big cowboy hat said as she thrust her hand out to greet me.

"Glad to meet you. I'm Allen and those are my granddaughters, Emily and Jessica."

"I'm the fourth hiker, Ray Rasmussen," a tall, middle-aged fellow with tousled brown hair said as we shook hands.

Dave came over and identified the wranglers who were busy packing and saddling the horses.

"That's Dave Carnell, a former park warden, and his wife, Anna, a former school teacher; Wendy Bush, a hiking guide and former dogsled outfitter; Hannah Grove, a pony trainer from England; Andy Roberto, my goddaughter who is a senior in high school; and Marilyn Manzer, my sister and our cook."

I unloaded our gear from the car and the wranglers packed it on the horses. Then Wendy introduced us to our horses.

"Emily," Wendy said, "you'll be riding Yeller."

"I'm Jessica," Jessica said. "She's Emily."

"Okay, Jessica, you'll be riding Yeller, and Emily, I think you should ride Pepper."

Wendy gave Jessica a boost up on Yeller, an 8-year-old golden palomino, and then helped Emily up on Pepper, a 6-year-old Appaloosa with tiny black spots on his backside. Wendy introduced me to Dancer, an 8-year-old Appaloosa, and I mounted up.

"Emily, I'd like you to ride in front of Pepper because Pepper likes to follow Yeller," Wendy said.

"I'm Jessica," Jessica corrected her again.

"Well, enough of that," Wendy said with a sigh. She grabbed two pieces of duct tape the wranglers were using to mark the weight on the pack boxes and wrote Emily and Jessica's names on them. Then she pasted the duct-tape nametags on the crown of the girls' hats so they were plainly visible. "Now I can tell you apart."

The four hikers and Gimli left early to hike to our first camp. It took until noon for the wranglers to get the horses packed. Finally, we started up the trail, Dave Carnell leading the packhorses and Jessica, Emily and I bringing up the rear with Wendy and Marilyn. Two other companions followed us: Happy, Marilyn's 30-pound female bearded collie; and Avery, Wendy's 80-pound black, male Chesapeake-Lab cross. About five minutes into the ride a tree branch knocked Jessica's hat off.

"Avery, search," Wendy commanded.

Avery ran up the trail looking for something that shouldn't be there. He found Jessica's hat and picked it up in his mouth.

"Avery, in my hand," Wendy said.

Avery came bounding back to Wendy, stood with his front paws on Wendy's horse's left shoulder and let Wendy take the hat out of his mouth.

"Good boy, Avery," Wendy complemented him and gave him a friendly pat on the head. Avery ran ahead wagging his tail.

As we crested the first big hill, I could look ahead and see the 34 horses of our packtrain winding their way down the hill in front of us. It looked like a scene out of a western movie, the packhorses jockeying for position, the wranglers shouting at them

The pack train stretched out like a John Wayne movie

to get back in line, Dave Manzer cracking his whip over their heads to get their attention and the beautiful, snow-covered Canadian Rocky Mountains ahead of us. This was shaping up to be the kind of adventure I hoped for.

Thirty minutes into the ride, a big mule deer stepped out of the forest, looked over the pack train and then, with four or five high arching leaps, bound back into the trees.

The trail led along the north side of the Wild Hay River, a clear, rapidly flowing stream about twenty or thirty feet wide. The trail itself was eight-to-ten feet wide, capable of supporting a team and wagon. Periodically we encountered a stream flowing into the Wild Hay and let the horses drink while crossing the stream.

Mid-afternoon we came to a small camp along the Wild Hay and stopped to eat. Lunch consisted of sandwiches Marilyn and Anna had made at the trail head, raw carrots, fruit and a candy bar. After lunch, Jessica had to go to the bathroom. There was no toilet in the camp so I took her to the edge of camp and told her to go behind a tree. Nearby stood a tree with a ladder attached and a platform about fifteen-feet up. Campers were supposed to store their food on the platform at night so the bears don't get it.

"Do I have to climb the ladder and pee up there?" Jessica asked wide-eyed.

"No, dear, you don't have to make a spectacle of yourself," I said.

"What's a spectacle?" Jessica asked.

"Just go behind the tree and go to the bathroom," I told her.

As we continued along the trail after lunch, I noticed terracing along the southfacing ridges. It looked like animals made parallel paths as they grazed on the side of the hills.

"That is called 'creep'," Dave Manzer told me. "One summer a geological team hired me to pack for them while they studied those ridges. They determined that the sun shining on the southfacing ridges thaws the top soil and it slides down or "creeps" and forms those ridges."

Wild flowers lined both sides of the trail: beautiful pink wild roses, brilliant red paintbrush, blue bells, purple fleabane, vivid yellow arnica and purple vetch.

About 7 o'clock we reached Eagle's Nest Camp, the first of five camps we would stay in, (see the map on page 17.) The hikers and pack train had arrived an hour before us. The horses were already in the corral and the tents set up. The wranglers ate their lunch along the trail so the packhorses didn't have to stand around with their heavy packs, and so they could get to camp before us to start getting supper ready. Emily, Jessica and I picked a large walled tent with a floor at the edge of camp. I retrieved our luggage from the pile and carried it to our tent. Jessica had an upset stomach so I fixed her air mattress and sleeping bag, gave her a Tylenol, some Pepto-Bismol and she went to sleep. Emily was talking with Andy, the 17-year-old high school student and Hannah, the 20-

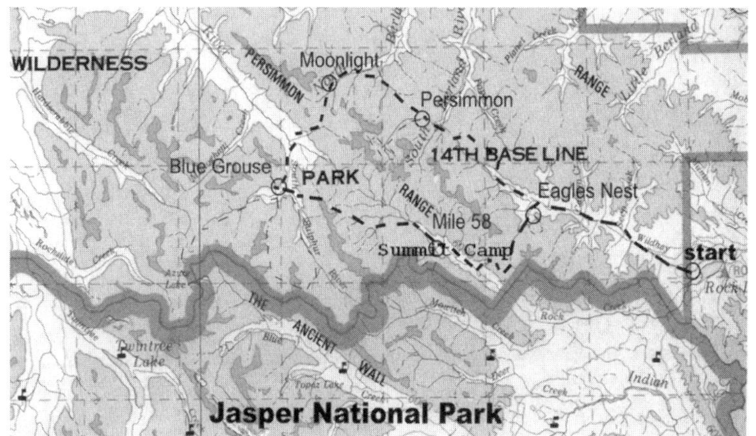

From Rock Lake we rode to five different camps

year-old British pony trainer. She quickly adopted them as her old sisters and followed them around all evening.

"How do you want your steak cooked?" Dave Manzer (M) asked as he tossed half a dozen T-bone steaks on the grill over a hot wood fire.

"Well done for me and for Emily," I said.

While the steaks were cooking, I went in the cook tent. The smell of onions frying and biscuits baking whet my appetite. Marilyn and Anna were busily working around the wood-fired cook stove which had a two-foot square cooking surface on top, a 5-gallon hot water tank on the left side and a large baking oven on the right side. Long tables lined the side of the tent with 14 pack boxes and up-ended cut logs for seats.

Dave came in with the first load of steaks and bid us to sit down and start eating while they were still hot.

"Would you like red wine or white with your steak?" Anna asked.

"I'll have white," I said, "and juice for Emily."

Marilyn dished out steaming corn-on-the-cob, baked potatoes, lettuce and tomato salad and fried onions while Anna set

17

Dave cooked steaks to order on the grill

the basket of hot biscuits on the table. Talk about roughing it, I hadn't eaten this well since my birthday dinner at the Paragon Restaurant last year. The steak was tender, juicy and delicious. The clear mountain air, smell of pine trees and long ride probably improved my appetite, but the meal turned out to be a super dining experience. No hotdogs roasted over an open fire on this trip. We topped supper off with fresh-baked apple pie and hot peppermint tea---a meal to write home about.

After supper we all sat around the campfire and watched the sun go down about 10 o'clock. Dave strummed his guitar and Marilyn sang as we soaked up the Willmore wilderness scenery. The shadows lengthened on the snow-capped mountains and the forest grew darker and darker green.

"I think it's bed time," I told Emily about 11 o'clock.

18

"Not yet, Grandpa," Emily objected. "I want to stay up and listen to Dave play."

"I'm going to unroll our mattresses and sleeping bags," I told her. "You come to bed pretty quick."

I fixed our sleeping bags, brushed my teeth and got ready for bed. Jessica continued to sleep soundly. Emily came in a few minutes later and got ready for bed.

"Did you have a good time today?" I asked.

"Yeah," Emily replied. "I love my horse and the people are so nice."

"This trip is starting out exactly as I hoped, beautiful wilderness, wild animals, adventure and good food. Good night," I said. Emily didn't answer, she had fallen asleep already. It was still light outside when I dropped off to sleep.

Chapter 4

If the Horse in Front of You Disappears in the Muskeg, Don't Go that Way

Clang, clang! Tinkle, tinkle! Clunk, clunk! The sound of horse bells ringing in the dark continued most of the night as five or six horses grazed around our tent. A sugar coating of frost covered the tent Wednesday morning. I had my head completely inside the sleeping bag and still felt cold all over. My Ohio sleeping bag wasn't designed for alpine temperatures. Even with my long underwear, pants, turtleneck pullover, wool shirt and socks on I still felt cold. I needed to come up with a different strategy to stay warm for the next 15 nights in the mountains.

The first light of dawn spilled over the eastern mountains and the moon sunk low on the western horizon as I pulled on my boots and jacket and unzipped the tent door. I saw Dave Carnell tying feed bags on the horses in the corral. He appeared to be the only one stirring at 5 a.m.

"What do you feed the horses?" I asked Dave.

"We feed them a little oats and some fortified pellets that contain grass and minerals," Dave said. "Some of the horses are a little skinny so I give them a little extra oats. The mules don't need any feed, except what they get grazing."

"Do you know all the horses by name?" I asked.

"Yeah," Dave replied. "If you're going to work with them, you'd better know them. Each horse or mule has a personality. Some are gentle and cooperative, others are sneaky and stubborn and a few are downright mean. Now Eeyore here is just plain lovable," Dave said as he tied the feed sack on a small, golden Fjord. "He'll do anything you ask of him and not complain."

The sun's first rays broke over the eastern mountains and lit up the distant snow-covered western mountains with a golden light that God only uses at dawn to welcome the new day. I walked over and sat down on a bench at the edge of camp overlooking the creek. The scene changed minute-by-minute as the rays crept steadily down the mountainside boulder-by-boulder. Wendy told me later that they refer to this time as the "magic hour." The smell of the spruce trees, the feel of the crisp mountain air and the tinkle of the horse bells added to the once-in-a-lifetime feeling I had as we started our Rocky Mountain adventure. I took out my notebook and started detailing our experiences from the previous day while they were still fresh in my mind. Occasionally I'd refer to the notes I'd taken as we rode along the trail to recall some exact details, the sequence of events or the names of the flowers we encountered.

I noticed Marilyn and Anna heading for the cook tent, and Wendy, Hannah and Andy helping Dave feed the horses. About the time I finished my notes, I smelled a delicious odor coming from the cook tent. I walked back to our tent to wake the girls.

"Sunrise in the swamp," I yelled. "Time to get up girls."

There was no sign of life in either sleeping bag. Both girls had their heads completely under the covers.

"Come on, girls. It's breakfast time."

"I'm cold," Emily complained from inside her sleeping bag.

"Me too," Jessica added from her bag.

"Get your boots and jackets on and we'll go down to the warm cook tent," I said.

Slowly a head appeared out of Emily's sleeping bag and then another one from Jessica's. I helped them get their jackets and boots on and they bolted out of our tent, ran up to the cook tent and huddled in front of the warm cook stove.

"Were you girls cold last night?" Anna asked.

"Yes," Emily and Jessica answered in unison.

"We'll have to do something about that tonight," Anna said. "I think we have an extra sleeping bag you can use. What would you like for breakfast?"

"Rice Krispies," they said.

Hannah had a collection of warm, furry hats

Anna gave them bowls, the Rice Krispies box and the milk container. They sat down at the table and ate a bowl of cereal.

"We've got French toast and sausage ready," Marilyn said as they finished their cereal.

Emily, Jessica and I got our plates and filed past the cook stove where Marilyn loaded them up with golden-brown French toast and sizzling link sausage. The hikers and wranglers started straggling in as Marilyn continued to dish out freshly cooked French toast. Dave Carnell sat across the table from me. He smothered his three slices of French toast with maple syrup and started eating the stack.

"I ended up with a lot of syrup," Dave said when he finished his French toast. "Marilyn, is there any chance I could have another stack of French toast to make the syrup come out even?"

"Sure," Marilyn said as she forked more French toast on his plate. Dave is a tall thin fellow, but a hearty eater.

Emily and Jessica finished off their French toast and then went outside to talk to the horses.

Jessica borrowed Hannah's brown beaver hat

"Fix yourself a lunch," Marilyn said as we finished breakfast. "There's lunch meat, peanut butter, cheese, salad, fruit and candy bars on the table."

I called the girls back in and we fixed our lunch. Then we took our lunches and full water bottles out and put them in our saddlebags.

About 10 o'clock the hikers headed off on a hike and we mounted up for a ride to Persimmon Ridge. Dave Manzer, Wendy and Hannah acted as our guides for the day. The temperature was still cold so Hannah loaned Emily and Jessica warm hats. Hannah has a thing for wooly hats. She wears a fur-lined leather hat with earflaps that snap under her chin. She also owns three or four other wooly hats. She loaned Emily a white sheepskin hat with the wool on the outside and Jessica a brown beaver hat. Wendy liked the idea because she could now recognize the twins by the different color hats.

We rode an eight-foot wide trail to camp the day before, but the paths we rode on this morning were twelve- to eighteen-inch

Emily borrowed Hannah's white sheepskin hat

wide game trails with grabby tree branches, scratchy bushes and tall prairie-grass. Dave loaned me a pair of chaps for the trip and I really needed them that day. My legs were continually getting poked with a branch, scratched with a wild rose bush or rubbed by three-inch saplings. Besides, the chaps kept my legs warm.

We rode across a meadow and then up the mountain through the thick, green forest. As we came down a draw, a tree had fallen across the trail. Emily and Jessica were in front of me and their horses stepped over the two-foot high log. My horse, Dancer, stopped, looked at the log, and then leaped over it with all four feet off the ground. The jump caught me completely by surprise. It felt like I was on a bucking bronco. I held on with my knees as both my arms flailed in the air, trying to find something to grab onto. Dancer came down with a thud and I threw my arms around his neck to keep from flying over his head.

"That was pretty neat," said Hannah who rode behind me. "Are you okay?"

"Yeah, I'm okay, but I really wasn't expecting him to leap over that log," I admitted.

"Grandpa," Emily said, "you should have expected it. His name is Dancer, not Stepper."

Smart aleck kids!

It started to rain as we continued up the mountain. When we left the protection of the spruce trees a cold wind hit me square in the face and the rain pounded down harder. My ears felt numb, my hands were wet and cold and I had no feeling in my toes. I felt miserable. "What are we doing up here?" I thought to myself. "As we climb higher it is just going to get colder and windier."

No one else complained so I kept my mouth shut and scrunched down in the saddle as our horses plodded up the hill. Ten minutes later we passed over a ridge and rode down to a mountain lake. The sun came out, the wind stopped and the temperature rose 20 degrees. I felt warm, dry and exhilarated with the magnificent view of the rugged snow-covered mountains, the clear blue lake and soft green grass.

"Let's eat lunch here," Dave suggested. We dismounted and broke out our lunches. I lay down in the soft grass and stared up at the craggy mountains wondering how many people turned back 500 yards short of this beautiful lake and missed this world-class scenery.

Wendy suggested Emily, Jessica and I join her for a hike around the lake. We jumped across the three-foot-wide stream and started around the lake. Near the mountain-end of the lake we encountered several huge chunks of the mountain shaped like perfect cubes, ten foot on a side. Emily and Jessica scampered up on top of one of the rocks with Avery right behind. After playing on the rock, they ran for the snowfield in the shadow of the mountain cliff. As Emily and Jessica threw snowballs, Avery jumped five feet into the air to catch them in his mouth. He didn't miss a single snowball. In between catches Avery would roll in the snow.

Emily and Jessica threw snowballs to Avery

The meadow around the lake was full of alpine flowers, not just one variety, but dozens of types: yellow mountain aven, bear root, heddi sarem, wolly louse wort, pink moss campion, white cotton grass, blue forget-me-nots, white heather, red columbine, white/yellow mountain daisies, yellow western buttercups, pink wild roses, white Labrador tea, yellow paintbrush, blue bells, blue lupines and purple mountain fleabane to name a few. A ten-foot by ten-foot area might contain six or seven different varieties of flowers. A fifty-foot diameter viewing circle might have twenty or twenty five different varieties. These mountains contain a complete botanical garden hidden in their sheltered valleys.

After exploring the lakeside for an hour or more, we wandered back to the horses and started our ride back to camp. The trail back went along the edge of the muskeg valley. Muskeg is a grassy bog or swamp that occurs in the northern mountains. The valley we followed had a 20-mile long muskeg swamp with only three safe crossing points. Even on the "good" trail, my horse would often sink a foot or two into the swamp in places. I hung on for dear life as Dancer staggered through the swamp.

"If you try to cross anywhere else," Dave cautioned us, "you're likely to sink in the swamp. Rumor is there's a horse, saddle and rider buried in the muskeg right about there," Dave said, pointing down the valley to the right. "I have one rule about riding through muskeg. If the horse and rider in front of you disappears, don't go that way!"

Emily and Jessica's riding ability amazed me. They maneuvered up and down steep gullies, through grabby willow thickets, over logs, under low-hanging branches and across streams like pros. They never complained of being sore or of having difficulties. They both climbed on and off their horses unassisted, a significant achievement since their stirrups hang at eye level to them. They mounted their horses by raising their left leg above their head and plant it in the stirrup. Then they grabbed the thongs attached to the front and back of the saddle, hung upside down and pulled themselves up into the saddle with their sheer strength. They looked like two gymnasts turning flips when they mounted their horses. To dismount, they held on the thongs and slid down the side of the horse.

"Your family looks like they have been riding forever," Ray Rasmussen commented when we rode back into camp.

The late afternoon turned sunny, calm and warm in camp, T-shirt weather. Supper was another culinary delight: baked six-layer lasagna, Caesar salad, hot garlic bread, red wine, fresh fruit and tea for dessert.

After supper Emily, Jessica and I played hide-and-seek in the meadow where the horses were grazing. I was it. The meadow bushed grew five-foot high and I never could find the girls hiding in the bushes. They would make noises to guide me toward them, but I could be five feet away from them and still not see them.

After 30 minutes of fruitlessly searching for them, I gave up and we started looking for the horses. The horses wore hobbles around their front feet so it was easy to catch up with them. Emily and Jessica wanted to pet all of them. Once Emily tried to walk up

Emily and Jessica roasted marshmallows most nights

to Black Jack, the mule, but he quickly hopped out of range braying at the top of his lungs and scaring Emily.

"Don't go near the mules," Dave cautioned the girls. "Mules are unpredictable animals. If a horse is treated right by one wrangler, it assumes everyone else is going to treat him that way and he's friendly toward everyone. Mules have to get to know each person individually. They don't assume anything. Even after they get to know you, they might kick you just for the fun of it. Mules are dangerous animals. Don't ever get within kicking range. If you have to walk around a mule, get his attention by talking to him before you go behind him so he knows you're there. Mules spook easily."

"Do you want to roast marshmallows?" Marilyn asked Emily and Jessica.

"Yeah!" they chimed together. "Can you cut us a stick, grandpa?"

Dave played the guitar and sang after supper

I cut two roasting sticks while Marilyn brought a bag of marshmallows the size of a ten-pound potato sack from the cook tent. Dave threw a few more pieces of wood on the fire. Emily and Jessica roasted at least two dozen marshmallows while Anna, Hannah and Wendy took turns reading "Treasure Island" out loud. The readers did so in character, imitating the gruff sounding pirates, the high-pitched voice of the kids and the deep voice of the adults. They read through three chapters before the twins filled up on marshmallows.

After the marshmallow roast, Dave played his guitar and sang. He had an amazing repertoire of songs: Puff the Magic Dragon, The Pony Man, Ghost Riders in the Sky, The Pickle Song and a dozen more. Anna entertained us with her fiddle playing and Marilyn and Lois played beautiful duet harmony on their recorders.

As we got ready for bed, I tried to figure out how to stay warm all night. Dave loaned us a heavy double sleeping bag. First, I put Emily and Jessica's sleeping bags inside the double bag. Then

I zipped their warm coats up and stuffed them down inside their bag.

"Put your feet inside your coats to keep them warm," I instructed them as they got into bed. "Wear all your clothes and the fuzzy hats Hannah loaned you." They snuggled down in their bags with just their noses sticking out.

"Will we smother if we cover our heads?" Emily asked.

"No. I sleep with my head under the covers all the time," I assured her.

I zipped my heavy jacket up and stuffed it down in my sleeping bag. Then I put on my light jacket, climbed in and tucked my feet inside my heavy jacket. Next I laid the empty, heavy duffel bag over my sleeping bag like a blanket. With my head tucked down inside the sleeping bag I was toasty warm. It took me about 60 seconds to fall asleep.

Chapter 5

Black Bear Cub

The frost sparkled in the bright moonlight when I got up at 5 a.m. No need for a flashlight, even though the sun was still an hour below the horizon. The moon lit up the forest with a soft, whitish glow revealing all the details of the camp. I made my way to the cook tent for a cup of tea. Wendy was just getting out of her sleeping bag and getting dressed.

"The staff tent was too noisy last night so I moved to the cook tent," Wendy explained.

Dave Carnell (C) already had a fire going in the cook stove and water heating for tea. As soon as the kettle started steaming, I filled the teapot. Between the warm cook stove and a hot cup of tea I soon felt toasty warm.

"So how did you get into the wrangling business?" I asked Wendy.

"I've always been interested in horses," Wendy said. "I was born and raised on a small gentleman's farm near Montreal in Quebec. My folks raised horses, chickens, ducks, geese and kids.

"Mother told me she took me for a horseback ride when I was three-months-old, and I've been around horses ever since," related Wendy. "My sister and brother couldn't help with the farm chores because of allergies so I ended up doing the heavy work. That's why I always say I'm the eldest 'son' in the family. Dad sent me to the University of Waterloo to become a biologist, but after a couple of years I decided to take some time off and head west. I worked as a dental assistant, but then ended up landing a week's work driving a dog team in a movie being filmed in Canmore. The movie starred Lee Marvin, Charles Bronson and Angie Dickinson. In three weeks of filming our dog teams managed 1.5 seconds of fame in the end, not much of a part!

Wendy, the head wrangler, is a tough lady with a soft-spot for children

"After that, I moved to Jasper and started working with the dogs. Jasper National Park banned the use of motorized vehicles in the backcountry, no skidoos or helicopters, so we pulled up the slack by hauling freight with the dog teams.

"I remember late one December there was a bunch of skiers who wanted to have a Christmas party at a lodge about twenty miles from the trail head. They hired us to haul all the food, drinks and decorations, about five hundred pounds of stuff. The temperature stood at minus twenty-five degrees Celsius (-13F) and the fresh snow was three-foot deep. My lead dog had to run loose to sniff out the hard packed trail buried under all that white stuff. Sometimes I had to snowshoe in front of the dogs to break the trail. Other times I lay down in the snow and tried to chew out the ice that built up between the sled dog's toes and their pads. I didn't think we were ever going to get to the lodge, but somehow we finally managed it.

"While I was raising the sled dogs, I wrote a book called 'Ascent of Dog – Working Dogs in the West.' It was finally published in 1998. I did get up to the Yukon once, to carry the mail with a real Canadian Mounted Policeman. We took the Mountie's dogs to Carcross, Yukon and with ten other teams traveled from there across Atlin Lake to Atlin, British Columbia, retracing an historic mail route. That was so much fun that for the last eight years my pinto team of horses and I have been carrying the mail once a year from Banff to High River, Alberta.

"I eventually gave up the dog business and enrolled in the University of Alberta to finish my degree. Then I moved back east to Toronto and lived on the 37th floor of a high-rise. For two and a half years I worked in customer service for Mountain Equipment Cooperative. I missed the horses, dogs and woods so I quit and moved to Banff to work for Parks Canada as a naturalist guide and information attendant in a federal government job. I've been doing that for ten years, but riding horses for Dave Manzer is way more fun. It may be a twelve-hour day, seven days a week job, but it's great being out in the mountains working with the horses and the mule train. I don't ever want to go back."

Emily and Jessica got up with the sun and came down to the cook tent to get warm. Marilyn fixed them a big helping of bacon and eggs for breakfast. The mountain air had given them a good appetite.

Today we broke camp to move across Eagle's Nest Pass to Summit Camp. It took about four or five hours to take down the tents, fold up the cook stove and pack 24 horses for the trip. The hikers took off after breakfast for Summit Camp. Emily, Jessica and I went for a walk in the meadow while the wranglers broke camp. We found a dry creek bed and played a "stay on the rocks" game. The game consisted of hopping from one large rock in the creek to another, never touching the sandy creek bed. Before hopping, I had to look ahead and see where to go from that rock so I didn't get stuck on a dead-end rock. We must have hopped a half-mile down the creek bed before the kids got tired of the game.

Then we played a "climb the sandy bank" game. The creek had eroded the bank of a 50-foot high sandy hill. We started climbing up the hill taking two steps up and sliding one step back in the loose sand. It took five minutes and a lot of effort to reach the top of the hill. Then we would run and slide down the hill taking seven-league strides, turn around and climb back up. Near the top Emily stepped on an anthill and a million mad ants came swarming out of their home. We stopped and watched as they scurried around, each carrying an egg or food. They appeared to be swarming around in a random pattern, but eventually got all their eggs and food moved to an undisturbed part of the anthill.

Starting back across the meadow, we encountered mountain ground squirrels, about the size of our ground hogs. The ground squirrels sat up on their hind legs to get a better look at us above the meadow grass. As we approached them, they dove back in their hole and disappeared down into below-ground tunnels. If we waited patiently, they would emerge from a different entrance and look at us.

Once back to camp, Wendy put the girls to work spreading out the canvas pack covers and holding the ropes as she made the packs for the horses. I helped Dave load the completed packs on the horses. Loading 4,000 pounds of equipment on 24 horses is hard work.

With the loading completed, we started up the Eagle's Nest Pass trail with our 34-horse train. The packhorses stretched a quarter-mile up the mountain trail through dark green spruce trees and up to the barren, snow-covered Canadian Rocky Mountains ahead. I couldn't believe I was really a part of it.

A short ways up the trail, we passed Cathedral Rock, a series of massive, fluted, limestone pillars.

"It would be fun to climb to the top of those rocks," I said to Dave.

"Not a good idea," Dave replied. "One of my wranglers climbed it last year and almost didn't get back down. It's all loose limestone. He said about every third rock he grabbed came loose and tumbled down the mountain."

The sky turned deep blue and cloudless as we followed the streambed over Eagle's Nest Pass. The temperature warmed up and we started peeling off layers of clothes. After reaching the saddle of the pass and starting down the other side, Emily, Jessica, Dave, Hannah and I turned off onto the high mountain trail while the rest of the wranglers and the packhorses continued down the main trail. A carpet of beautiful wildflowers covered the southfacing mountainside: blue forget-me-nots, purple larkspur, blue speedwell, purple Jacob's ladder, pink heather, white mountain daisies and a strange little pink flower called elephant head. The elephant head grows on a long stalk with a cluster of flowers on top. Each flower resembles an elephant head complete with big ears and a long, curved trunk.

The moon rose over the mountains in the afternoon

"These are black bear tracks," Dave said pointing to huge, deep depressions in the muddy trail. "And these look like mountain lion tracks," he said, pointing to smaller, four-toed tracks.

"What should we do if we encounter a grizzly bear?" I asked.

"Nothing," Dave replied. "Just stand still, keep quiet and the bear will leave when he sees or smells you. We've never had a report of anyone being killed by a grizzly in Willmore. The bears here are omnivores. They occasionally dig up a ground squirrel, but their main diet is roots and berries. A bear can eat 100,000 berries in a day. I call their droppings berry pies."

We stopped in a grassy meadow by a stream and ate our lunch. Dave asked Jessica to refill his water bottle from the stream. The streams are so clean in Willmore that you don't need iodine

We rode on game trails through the mountains

tablets or water purification kits, just drink the water as it comes.
None of us got sick from the stream water during the entire trip.

Jessica and Emily crossing the West Sulphur River

As we started down a valley, I noticed a line of dead trees marking the edge of an old forest fire.

"These dead spruce trees can stand for hundreds of years," Dave explained. "One year I outfitted for some park rangers who were doing a study on the age of the various burns in Willmore. They could tell the age of a burn by taking a core from the new-growth trees and measuring their age. It takes a few years after a burn before anything starts growing here. The new-growth pine trees here are about six-feet high. This burn occurred in 1951 and was the most recent one in Willmore. If you notice, most of the old tree trunks are not burned at all. The fire burns the needles and branches and then the tree dies."

About that time a brown spruce grouse (a chicken-sized bird with feathers extending down their legs to their feet) darted out

Jessica and Yeller disappearing in the willows

of the underbrush, followed by her two small chicks. They scampered down the trail and then disappeared back into the underbrush. A few minutes later another grouse flew up from beside us and landed off to the side of the trail. Continuing along the mountain stream, we encountered a solid wall of willow trees.

"After a burn, the willows take over," Dave said. "They don't have any competition from the taller trees so they grow profusely."

Twelve-foot high willows had completely overgrown the trail. By looking at the ground I could see where the trail used to be, but at horse-head level, there was no opening at all. Jessica rode about ten feet in front of me; she would disappear, swallowed up by the willow branches. The willow branches scraped along the sides of the horses and across my legs. Thank heaven for the chaps. There was no way to push individual branches out of the way as we plowed through so I just clasped my hands together like praying and protected my face as the horse plowed through the thick willows.

Jessica spotted the bear cub with its paw in the snare

"Damn!" Dave yelled as he came to an abrupt stop in the willow fifteen feet in front of me. "I've got my foot caught in something. It's a damn snare! It about jerked me out of my saddle."

We sat in the willows for a minute until Dave got his foot out of the snare loop and pried the snare wire off the tree.

"There's a bear!" Jessica said, pointing up the trail. About thirty feet ahead a little black bear cub lay on the ground with its paw up in the air.

"Everyone stay where you are," Dave said as he moved forward slowly to examine the bear. "It's okay, he's dead."

We rode out of the willows and dismounted near the bear. The bear cub had its right paw caught in a wire snare, which was anchored about five-foot up on a tree stump.

"The bear hasn't been here long," Dave said. "He hasn't started to decompose. I'll call the rangers about this when we get to camp."

Emily and Jessica were upset at seeing the bear cub in the snare.

"They shouldn't do this to a bear cub," Emily said.

"You're right," I agreed. "It's against the law and very cruel."

(Dave did call the park rangers that night using his satellite phone. The rangers came out and removed the cub. After finding other illegal snares and bait in the area, they talked to the local trapper who had a cabin in that area and he denied the snares were his. The rangers said they couldn't do anything more about it. One of our hikers, Ray Rasmussen, reported the incident to the Edmonton Journal and they wrote a front-page story on September 14, 2003, about how budget cuts at the Fish and Wildlife Service had reduced the patrols and enforcement of the game laws.

"We've lost twenty-five grizzly bears this year to poachers," the director of an environmental group said, "and most of the cases have never been solved because the government lacks resources to enforce the laws.")

After taking a few photos of the bear, we continued down the mountain and rejoined the main trail in the valley. Dave asked if we'd like to walk awhile. After six hours on the horses, it felt good to stretch our legs. We walked with the horses for about 15 minutes and then mounted up and rode into camp.

The wranglers and hikers were already in camp. Emily and Jessica helped me carry our sleeping bags and luggage to our tent. It was 9:30 p.m. by the time we got around to supper—very continental. We dined on tender roast chicken, white rice with a delicious wild cranberry gravy and fresh broccoli salad—mouth-watering.

After supper, everyone was tired except Emily and Jessica. I went to bed about 10:30 p.m. with the sun still shining on the mountains. Emily and Jessica promised they would come to bed soon, as they sat around the campfire talking with the wranglers.

"Aren't you girls tired?" Wendy asked with a yawn.

"No," Emily replied. "Grandpa said we could stay up until you guys went to bed."

"Well, I'm going right now," Wendy announced.

Reluctantly, Emily and Jessica brushed their teeth and came to bed. We arranged their sleeping bags inside the double sleeping bag and stuffed their coats down to keep their feet warm. They put their fuzzy hats on and snuggled down inside their toasty-warm nest. I didn't hear another sound out of them all night.

Chapter 6

Grizzly Bears

"Where's Eeyore?" Wendy asked Dave Carnell when he came back from rounding up the horses.

"I thought he was in camp," Dave said. "I didn't see him out in the meadow."

"He's not here," Wendy said. "I haven't seen him since we fed the horses last night."

"I found Eeyore," Anna yelled. "He's in the feed tent."

"How did he get in there?" Wendy asked. "It's been zipped up all night."

"He was inside with the door zipped up," Anna replied. "I don't know how he did it, but he got in and zipped the door closed."

"Nah," Wendy said. "Eeyore is clever, but he's not that clever."

"Where is my blue jacket?" Jessica asked. "I left it by the campfire last night and it's gone."

"My coat is missing too," Andy said. This was the day for losing things.

We looked in our tent, the cook tent, in Jessica's saddlebags, around the campfire—everywhere for fifteen minutes before we gave up. An hour later when Dave started saddling the horses we found Jessica's and Andy's coats on the saddle rack under the tarp. Someone had gathered up all the loose coats laying around the campfire the night before and put them under the tarp to keep them from getting wet if it rained.

After breakfast we rode up to Desolation Pass. The overgrown trail passed through a marsh and a meadow. My legs continually scraped willows and thorny bushes as I parted the thick underbrush. Thank heaven for the chaps!

"There's a white-crowned sparrow," Ray said, pointing to a small, brownish bird sitting on top of a small willow tree. It had

We rode up the valley toward Desolation Pass

a black head and three white stripes running across its crown. "Listen to its song."

"Bring me Cheesies, please," the white-crowned sparrow sang over and over. Its song consisted of a musical, rising two-note beginning followed by a high, buzzy "chee-zee-zee" and a trill.

We continued up the valley, climbing higher and higher. Then we rode up on a mile-long, 500-foot high knoll and stopped for lunch. Walking around the top of the knoll, Emily spotted a Jasper National Park sign on a post.

"We're right on the edge of Jasper National Park," Dave Carnell told Emily and Jessica. "There's a $10 fee for entering the park. If you walk past that sign, I'll have to collect $10 from each of you and send it to the Park," Dave joked.

"I ain't paying," Jessica said as she stepped beyond the sign and quickly jumped back.

"There's a caribou," Dave Manzer said as he scanned the mountain with his binoculars. "It looks like a pretty big bull standing

Movement of the earth's crust formed a beautiful folded pattern in the mountains

in that pile of snow. The caribou can't take the heat of summer and they often find a snow bank to cool off in."

We each took turns looking at the caribou through the binoculars. It was a half-mile away and hard to find in the seven-power Canon binoculars. These binoculars had a motion stabilization feature that allowed me to find the caribou, press the stabilization button and freeze the image. Without the stabilization, the image jumped all around my field of view. Great invention!

From the top of the knoll, I could see a beautiful fold pattern in the side of the mountain. Thin sedimentary layers of the earth which once were flat, curved into a giant letter "C" (laying on its side) as the earth's crust shifted and the mountain pushed up.

"Wonder if that's a bear or a black rock," Dave Carnell said, pointing to a meadow a mile away as we rode down the knoll. "If it's still in the same spot when we crest the next hill, we'll know it's a rock," he said.

Dave spotted a caribou cooling off near a snow patch

Cresting the next hill, we could make out a sow grizzly bear and twin bear cubs half a mile away walking across the meadow and heading for a deep draw. A minute later they disappeared down into the draw. We continued riding toward them. About that time we saw Ray walking up the next hill, just above the draw where the bears disappeared. After lunch, Ray decided to hike back to camp rather than ride and he left before us. Dave yelled at Ray and got his attention. Then he motioned for him to wait for us so he wouldn't walk over the hill and encounter the bears.

Ray waited as we rode down one hill and up the next. Then we all continued slowly up the hill and to the edge of the draw. The sow bear stood a scant 100 feet away on the other side of the draw with her twin cubs. As I took photos, the bear started digging into the hillside after a ground squirrel. The dirt flew from the bear's gigantic paws like a Ditch Witch running in high gear. In minutes she had moved half a ton of soft dirt and had a five-foot diameter cave dug five-foot deep. Mama bear finally reached the squirrel's den and the frightened squirrel shot out between the bear's legs like greased lightning. The sow reared up on her hind legs, swirled around and dove through the air for the squirrel. Her paws clamped around it as her 500-pound body bounced down the hillside. The bear quickly scooped the squirrel into her mouth and I could hear an audible "crunch" as she put it out of its misery. Mama then carried the limp ground squirrel back up to her cubs and laid it between them. The cubs started at opposite ends and all signs of the plump ground squirrel disappeared in a few seconds. The entire episode took ten minutes and seemed like a National Geographic Special.

The bear took no notice of the dozen people, 12 horses and 3 dogs that watched her from the hill 100 feet away. Dave Manzer decided to get her attention since we planned to ride down through the draw she occupied. He started whistling and yelling and the bear looked up the hill at us. She just stood still, assessing the situation. Finally, Dave cracked his whip and the bear decided to

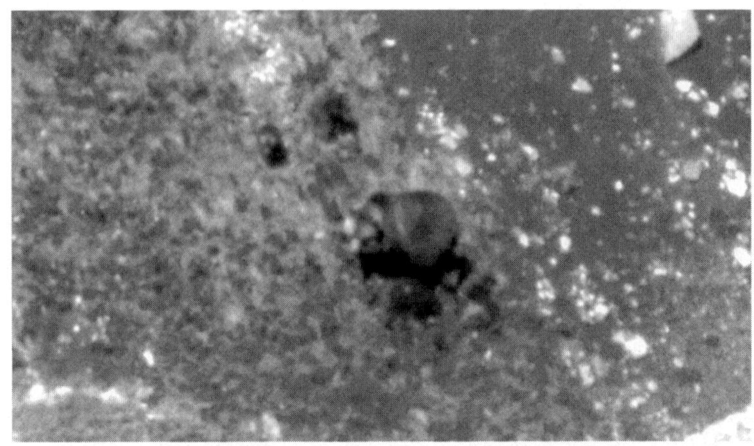

The sow bear dug up a ground squirrel for her cubs

move away. She walked slowly up the draw away from us with her cubs running behind. Every time Dave cracked his whip, the bear would stop, turn around and look at us as if to say, "I'm not afraid of you." Then she'd turn back around and continue up the draw. We waited until she walked out of sight before starting through the draw.

Rather than ride down the draw where the bear disappeared, Dave elected to ride up the other side and cross over the top of the hill. The side of the draw consisted of loose rock or scree and made poor footing for the horses. Dancer slipped and slid as he carried me up the side of the draw. The path Dave chose followed a small dry creek that flowed down the side of the draw. Wendy rode Ernie just in front of me as we climbed up the steep, loose hillside. All of a sudden, Ernie's right hind foot slipped on the scree and his entire hind end started sliding down into the brushy ravine. Wendy dove off the left side of the horse into the scrub brush while a thousand pounds of horseflesh tried to paw the air to keep from falling into the ravine. In a matter of seconds, Ernie slid down the ravine on his back with his four feet flailing through the air. He finally hit the bottom of the ravine and lay on his side with his feet pointed up the

The boar bear lay in a draw two hundred yards from us

ravine, kicking frantically to try to right himself. Wendy sprinted down to Ernie and tried to calm the wild-eyed horse. Once he stopped struggling, she helped him roll over with his feet down the hill so he could get up. Then she led him back up to the trail.

"Could you do that again?" I joked as Wendy dusted herself off. "I'd like to take pictures."

"Keep your camera ready," Wendy advised. "It could happen again before we get to the top of the hill."

As we crested the hill and started down the other side, Dave Carnell pointed out another bear.

"He's up in that wash, about 200 yards away," he said.

Dave Manzer took his binoculars out and looked at the bear.

"It's a big grizzly boar," Dave said. "He's just laying there."

"Could he be the father of the cubs?" I asked.

"Could be, but boars don't usually stay around after the cubs are born," Dave said. "They're not very good fathers. They try to eat the cubs."

"I've been coming out here eight weeks a year for five summers," Marilyn said, "and those are the first grizzlies I've ever seen. You guys come up here and see four grizzlies on your first trip. Boy, are you lucky."

Starting down the hill, we came to a scree field that stretched 200 feet across the hill and extended all the way down the mountain.

"We'll ride across single file at a shallow angle," Dave advised. "If your horse starts to slide, jump off."

Very slowly we crossed the scree field --- no problem. Toward the bottom of the hill, we reached the tree line and entered the forest with no trail. Dave guided us as we picked our way through the hilly forest, climbing over downed trees, pushing through prickly pine trees that grew shoulder to shoulder with no room between. It proved to be the very definition of bushwhacking (to clear a path through a thick forest of bushes and low-hanging branches.) I had to continuously ward off flying limbs and body-gouging dead branches as Dancer crashed down the hillside. I watched in amazement as Emily and Jessica fought their way down the steep hill through the brambles, never complaining, never whining and never giving up. Those 50-pound girls had full control of their 1,000-pound mounts.

We arrived back at camp about 7 p.m. Jessica and I opted for a hot shower. Emily decided to take her shower in the morning. The shower hangs in a six-foot square tent. I filled the water container with five gallons of hot water from the cook stove and hung it from the hook at the top of the tent. Jessica took her shower first, Army style. Run enough water to get wet and then stop the water. Soap up good and then run the water again to rinse off. The steamy hot water felt great and there was a temptation to stand and soak, but unfortunately, there wasn't enough hot water for that— just enough to get clean and get out.

We bushwhacked down through the thick brush

After I finished my shower, I watched Dave grill huge salmon filets on the campfire. Supper consisted of tender grilled salmon on a bed of steaming pasta noodles, hot corn on the cob, a crisp Greek salad and cranberry cheesecake for dessert—delicious. Emily and Jessica went back for a second helping of salmon. An eight-hour horseback ride through the mountains gave them a big appetite.

As we sat around the dinner table drinking our tea, Ray showed us a softball-sized meteorite he found on the trail in Desolation Pass. It was extremely heavy, obviously solid iron. It had odd marble-sized bumps all over it as though it was composed of nodules fused together.

"How long have you been coming to Willmore?" I asked as I passed the meteorite back to Ray.

"About 25 years," Ray said. "I started hiking here back in the 1970s. I've come back with hiking groups or by myself almost every year."

"What do you do for a living?"

"I'm more or less retired now, but I have a computer and business background. I taught Leadership, Business Teamwork and Team Building at the University of Alberta, Edmonton."

"Have you always used Dave as an outfitter?"

"No, I just started using Dave eight or nine years ago," Ray said. "I used various other outfitters before that, including George Kelley and Scary Gary, but I like Dave best."

Ray was the strongest hiker in our group and sometimes hiked the longer, harder trails by himself when the other hikers decided to ride on one of the day trips or take a day off. He is also an excellent photographer with the patience to wait for the animals to move into the most photogenic pose before taking his pictures. He has a website (http://raysweb.net) with hundreds of beautiful photos of animals, flowers and wilderness scenes.

Ray was the most experienced hiker on the trip

After supper, Emily and Jessica roasted marshmallows over the campfire. Anna showed them how to warm the marshmallow up and make it pliable.

"Then you smoosh it in your fingers until it gets like toffee," Anna demonstrated. "Once it is pliable you can make the alphabet with it, one letter at a time." Anna worked her marshmallow until it resembled the letter H. Then she coached Emily and Jessica as they tried to make various letters. The smooshy marshmallow survived for about five minutes as the kids made letters resembling H, E, W, O, I, A, T and U. Then they ate the sticky marshmallow off their fingers and started out with a new one. Who needs TV when you can make a marshmallow alphabet?

"Anyone want to play dominos?" I asked.

"Sure," Andy agreed. "I love playing games. Did you bring dominos?"

"I just happen to have a set of double-12s with me," I said as I dug out the five-pound metal box. Emily, Jessica, Andy, Wendy and Mark joined me. "We'll play a version called Mexican Train."

We played a serious game of double-12s dominos

I explained the rules as we each drew 14 dominos and started playing. The game didn't demand too much concentration so there was plenty of time to talk, joke and tell stories.

"The Mexican train I'm familiar with was a little more ominous," Wendy said. "I went south of the border a few years ago and took the train across Mexico. As we passed through a small village in the mountains, the train stopped and a bunch of Federalies climbed on board, armed to the teeth. They started going through the train, car by car, strip-searching all the men, looking for drugs. The Mexican lady sitting across from me motioned for me to come and sit next to her. 'Tenga ojo' (have eyes---watch out) she said, poking her two fingers toward her eyes in pantomime. She continued to knit and I hid my face in a magazine as the Federalies passed our row and hauled off the guys in the next row. They never bothered us."

The dominos game broke up about 11 p.m. and I went to bed.

"Isn't it time for you girls to get your PJs on?" Wendy asked Emily and Jessica. The staff was tired and ready for bed, but Emily and Jessica were still bouncing off the wall. They only have two speeds---fast forward and stop dead. They came back to our tent and fell asleep 60 seconds after their heads hit the pillows.

Chapter 7

The Surprise Party

The wranglers stood in a tight knot inside the cook tent apparently plotting some mischief when I came in searching for a cup of tea Saturday morning.

"We'll put up balloons and flags," Wendy said.

"I'll bake the birthday cake," Andy said.

"I've got candles," Anna chimed in.

"What's going on?" I asked.

"It's Dave Manzer's birthday and we're planning a surprise party for him," Hannah said.

Marilyn (Dave's sister) came in the tent and asked what they were doing.

"We're planning a surprise birthday party for Dave," Dave Carnell said.

"It'll be a really big surprise since his birthday is in December," Marilyn said with a laugh. "You could make it a surprise anniversary party for Mark and Lois. This is their 25th wedding anniversary."

"Great idea," Wendy said. "I'll make a big banner out of a couple of feed sacks."

"We could have everything up and in place when Mark and Lois come back from their hike this afternoon," Anna suggested. The committee agreed and each started preparing their part of the decorations.

Breakfast turned out to be another culinary delight. Fluffy, golden pancakes filled with plump, sweet strawberries, peaches, grapes, bananas and blackberries, and topped with real maple syrup and blueberry yogurt. Emily and Jessica showed their approval by going back for more pancakes and more yogurt.

After breakfast I attended to my household chores, washing out some of Emily's and Jessica's dirty clothes. My first inclination was to wash them in the creek. Wendy advised against doing that.

"The creek is our drinking water. Use a bucket."

I filled a bucket with hot water and washed the clothes using Tide I brought for that purpose. After five minutes of sloshing the clothes in the bucket, I wrung them out and sloshed them some more. It took two rinsings with warm water and one with cold water to get all the suds out of the clothes. Then I wrung them out and hung them over the tent support ropes to dry.

"You should teach the girls to do their own laundry," Wendy scolded me as I hung Emily's jeans on the line. "I'll give them a lesson tonight," Wendy promised.

Dave M worked on his whip after breakfast. He cut a new piece of leather for the end and attached a short piece of binder's twine on the tip.

"I have to replace the tip every second or third day," Dave said. "The cracking sound is made when the tip goes super sonic and it doesn't take many cracks to tear the tip up."

Wendy braided Emily and Jessica's hair and gave them red head scarves covered with Canadian maple leaves. They looked very Canadian as we headed out for our day's ride to Cannonball Meadow.

The trail led through a big meadow and a series of muskeg bogs. The horses sunk down a foot deep into the muskeg as they weaved back and forth, skirting the edge of the bogs.

"How do you know where it's safe to ride?" I asked Dave M.

"Where there's a willow, there's a way," Dave said. "The willows won't grow in the real soft part of the muskeg, and the willow roots help hold the muskeg together."

"Why do they call this Cannonball Meadow?" I asked.

"You ask an awful lot of questions," Dave said with a laugh. "Are you writing a book or something?"

"Yeah," I replied.

"Well, apparently a bunch of small meteorites landed here during a meteor shower," Dave said. "According to the old timers, cannonball-sized meteors could be found all through this valley. It's rare to find one today—too many people already been up here looking for them."

We rode up above the tree line and to the top of a half-mile long knoll. White, bleached caribou bones littered the side of the trail. From the top of the knoll three sparkling waterfalls could be seen splashing down the side of the snow-covered mountain in front of us. Time for a lunch break and rest at top of the knoll.

"Happy's got something!" Emily hollered as Marilyn's dog came bounding up the hill with a fuzzy tail sticking out of her mouth.

"Come here, Happy," Marilyn said as she climbed down from her horse. "What did you catch?"

"It's a golden-mantle ground squirrel," Wendy said as she took it from her.

The squirrel-sized animal looked like a big chipmunk with two white stripes running from head to hips, bordered by black. The rest of the squirrel's back was salt-and-pepper gray.

"Is it going to be okay?" Jessica asked.

"No," Wendy said, "its back is broken. I'm going to have to send it off to ground-squirrel heaven." She walked over to the side of the knoll, dispatched the squirrel and buried it under a rock so none of the dogs would dig it up. Emily and Jessica picked a bouquet of wild flowers and placed them on the grave stone.

"I hope the squirrel has a nice rest and comes back as something else," Emily said.

"That's the first time Happy has ever caught anything," Marilyn said, "and I hope it's the last time."

After, I wandered around this very prolific mountain garden counting the different alpine flowers growing there:

Yellow western buttercups

White wild strawberry flowers

We rode to the top of the ridge for lunch and a view

Purple moss campion
Western anemone
Blue lupines
Pink heather
Blue forget-me-nots
Purple silky phacelia
Wooly louse wart
Yellow cinquefoil
Purple fox gloves
Blue larkspur
and a dozen I couldn't name (see Appendix D for a complete list of flowers identified on the trip).

We rode down the hill and back below the tree line into a forest of pine, spruce, poplar, birch, willow and balsam.

"The balsam doesn't burn worth a darn," Dave said while passing through a thick stand of balsam trees. "This area is called

59

We could see 50 miles in all directions from the knoll

the 'moose farm' because back in the 1950s, you'd see 50 or 60 moose as you rode through this area. They're all gone now. I've never seen a moose on the 'moose farm' in the 25 years I've been coming up here."

The trail led down the mountain, past some rock slide areas where the debris piled up into mounds that looked like a truck had backed up and dumped a load of gravel there. We arrived back in camp tired after the seven-hour ride, but not sore.

Marilyn, Wendy and Hannah hung up the "Happy Anniversary" banner, the flags and the balloons before Mark and Lois got back from their hike. As they walked up the trail into camp we all yelled, "Happy Anniversary!"

"This is a pleasant surprise," Mark said. "I never expected anyone would throw us a surprise anniversary party out here in the wilderness."

"We even baked you a cake," Marilyn said as she and Hannah served the coffee and cake.

Mark & Lois celebrated their 25th wedding anniversary

"How did you two meet?" I asked while eating the delicious cake.

"I teach canoeing and outdoor activities at a college in Edmonton," Mark said. "Lois took my canoeing course. After the course, I asked her to do some secretarial work for the White Water National Championship races we run. One thing led to another and after a couple of years we married. We've been married 25 years. This trip is our anniversary present to each other."

"Do you have any children?"

"Yes," Lois answered. "We have two sons, Eric 23 and Hans 18, and a daughter, Anna 21."

"What do you do for a living?"

"I teach music to kindergarten through sixth grade in Edmonton. I'm also active in a bell ringer's choir. In our spare time Mark and I do a lot of camping, canoeing and hiking."

Wendy filled the wash bucket with warm water before supper and asked Emily and Jessica to get their dirty clothes. Then she coached them as they scrubbed, rinsed, wrung out and hung their clothes up to dry.

"Now your grandpa won't have to do your laundry anymore," Wendy said.

A bolt of lightning lit up the camp like a giant flash bulb as we sat around the campfire talking after supper. The thunder cracked a few seconds later, indicating the lightning hit less than a mile away. Emily jumped into my lap and Jessica into Wendy's lap. They're afraid of lightning and thunder. A minute later Dave C, Anna and Andy rode into camp. They had ridden to our next camp, Blue Grouse, to drop off some tents and supplies.

"That lightning hit right alongside the trail," Anna said. "Scared me, but it didn't spook the horses."

To calm the twins Dave M started playing his guitar and Marilyn joined in with her recorder. Emily requested the "Pony Man" and Jessica requested the "Pickle Song." Dave played and sang for an hour. He used to play professionally in nightclubs in his youth and knew hundreds of songs. Emily and Jessica sang along with him after hearing the songs a few nights before. Dave and Marilyn's father was a social worker and he used to play an album of weird songs about being psychoanalyzed and treated for mental disorders. Dave and Marilyn sang several of the songs from that album including "Gunslinger." Emily and Jessica liked that song and kept asking Dave to sing it again.

Chapter 8

To the Warden with the Horse and Dog on Skyline Trail

At night the horses were hobbled and let loose in the meadow to graze. By morning some of them have strayed miles from camp. Two of the wranglers usually round them up, but Wendy said I could go along with Dave Carnell this morning since I needed some more "adventure" material for the book. Dave and I rode out of camp at dawn to round up the horses.

Some of the mules and horses had already wandered into camp looking for breakfast, but a dozen of the more independent ones were still hiding in the meadow. Each horse had a bell around its neck so by stopping and listening we could figure out where they were hiding. We found three of the palominos first and got them started back toward camp. Next Dave located several mules and headed them home. Abelard and Heloise were eating the fresh grass by the edge of the stream. Dave circled around them and coaxed them back toward camp. Yeller and Pepper had strayed the furthest from camp, about two miles. We finally located them, took their hobbles off and drove them in front of us back toward the camp. While crossing a two-foot wide stream, Dancer caught me by surprise again by jumping high in the air. The two-G acceleration when he started the jump and zero-G as he came back down felt very exhilarating. I should have assumed Dancer would jump rather than step over even the smallest obstacle.

Marilyn and Anna served us a delicious cheese omelet, toasted English muffins and blackberry jam for breakfast. I don't know how Marilyn manages to pack 20 dozen eggs on those bucking mules without having most of them broken by the time we get to camp.

Moving day. The hikers took off after breakfast for our next camp. I helped Wendy take down the shower tent and held up some of the packing boxes as she lashed them to the horses. Then

Emily, Jessica and I sat down to read a book Anna gave us called *Stone Fox*, by John Gardiner.

The story related how little Willy entered a dogsled race with his dog named Searchlight to win enough money to keep his grandfather from losing their farm to the tax man. Emily and Jessica each read a chapter and then I read one in turn. I ended up reading the last chapter. As the dogsleds rounded the final turn and headed for the finish line, Willy and Searchlight had a considerable lead, but the Indian called Stone Fox and his four white Samoyeds were coming up fast. As Stone Fox pulled up alongside Willy, Searchlight sensed the challenge and summoned every ounce of strength to pull ahead again. One hundred feet from the finish line, Searchlight's heart burst and she fell. The sled and Willy tumbled over her. (I had to pause for a minute at that point in the story. I got a lump in my throat and tears in my eyes. After regaining my composure, I finished reading the story.) Stone Fox stopped his team behind Willy, took out his rifle, fired a shot in the air and announced that if any of the other racers tried to pass Willy, he'd shoot them. Then Willy carried Searchlight across the finish line and saved the farm.

As we waited for the wranglers to finish packing the horses, Anna suggested the girls make a 'dream catcher.' I cut two supple willow branches and Anna showed Emily and Jessica how to bend the sticks into a loop and weave a dream catcher with twine. The girls spent an hour making their dream catcher frames and then they started decorating them with feathers, horsehair, tufts of mountain-goat fur and pretty flowers. They added special mementos to their dream catchers over the following two weeks and had very unique designs to take home and show their mom.

As another part of my "adventure" package, I got to ride at the front of the pack train this day to experience leading 34 pack and riding horses. In some western movies you see the packhorses tied together. That might work if you were going across a flat desert, but not with the steep hills, narrow wooded trails and deep streams we crossed. All 34 horses/mules were loose and kept in

Anna showed the girls how to make dream catchers

line by the constant yelling, whip cracking and coercing of the seven wranglers.

The wranglers kept up a constant chatter, praising the horses that respond, cussing the ones that try to stray and occasionally riding off to coax one back in line. One of the young mules, Black Jack, apparently decided he should lead the pack and if anyone else got in front of him he would nip, kick and bray until he got back in the lead. Dave M said the horses and mules didn't respond to their names, just to the loud commands, but when Wendy, Anna or Hannah addressed a particular animal by name, its ears would perk up and it would usually fall back in line. Anna and I rode point for most of the way and sometimes I was left in front by myself while Anna galloped off, cracking her whip and yelling at Black Jack, Willy or Buckwheat to get back in line. Riding point is hard work and finally got approval to travel to Canada for the purpose of marrying dad. They got married and moved to Alberta where dad and his brother bought a farm and raised potatoes. They had a bumper crop, but so did everyone else so they couldn't sell them. He left the farm requires constant attention. Anna seemed to have eyes in the back of her head. She could watch the trail ahead and still sense when one of the mules started acting up behind her.

Everyone wore their Snowy River slickers because it rained off and on all day. It had rained hard up in the mountains and the streams ran high and fast. While crossing a two- or three-foot deep stream, Avery got caught in the turbulent water and started floating down stream. Jessica moved her horse into the middle of the stream to catch him. He clung to the upstream side of Yeller near Jessica's stirrup as she urged her horse across the swollen stream. When they got to the bank where Avery could touch bottom, he scampered up the bank, shook the icy water off, barked a thank you to Jessica and ran to catch up with Wendy.

Mid-day, Victor, one of the fjord, decided to buck his pack off, just for fun. Dave C and Hannah rounded him up and we all stopped while they repacked him. Emily and Jessica said their feet were cold so Wendy had them dismount, run down to the end of the meadow, pick a bouquet of wild flowers and run back. That warmed them up and we all started out for camp as soon as they got back on their horses.

Passing through a patch of willows, a mama grouse and two chicks flew up and landed in the trees. Two other chicks ran down the trail ahead of me for a hundred yards before darting off to the side and disappearing in the thick brush. It seemed odd that the dogs didn't chase the grouse.

As Anna and I rode point she told me a little about herself.

"My mom and dad were born in different parts of Denmark and never met each other there," Anna said. "In 1945, at the end of the war, they separately immigrated to Iceland. They met at a social gathering arranged by the Danish community there. Dad had applied for a visa to Canada and it came through so he came here. Mom applied for a visa and finally got approval to travel to Canada for the purpose of marrying dad. They got married and moved to Alberta where dad and his brother bought a farm and raised potatoes. They

Avery almost got swept away in the turbulent stream

Anna is a hearty Scandinavian lady with a heart of gold
had a bumper crop, but so did everyone else so they couldn't sell
them. He left the farm and started working as a carpenter. They
bought five acres, built a house and started raising a family. We
rode in the local pony club as children. Our favorite horse was a
bombproof 29-year-old gentleman who liked eating pies cooling in
the kitchen window. Dad died in 1990, but my mom is still living
near Calgary."

"When did you meet Dave?" I asked.

"I just met him a few years ago," Anna said. "I grew up
near Calgary and loved to play the piano. I dreamed of being a
concert pianist and conductor. However, I loved books as much as
music so I followed my dad's advice to do music for the love of it
and become a teacher/librarian instead. I went to the University of
Calgary and earned a Bachelor's Degree in Education. I love to
travel so my girl friend and I took a couple of years off and went to

Anna and Jessica took turns fixing each other's hair

New Zealand and Australia to work and travel. After that, we continued up to Malaysia and then over to Europe. We bummed around Europe for awhile and then worked as the cook's helpers on a ship to get to Iceland. We worked in a fish-processing factory in Iceland for awhile and finally flew home to Canada.

"Then I went to work in the elementary grades as a teacher and librarian. About seven years ago my girl friend and I took a holiday hiking through Jasper National Park. The weather was terrible: cold, rainy and windy. After one night in a leaky tent we were soaked, bedraggled and cold so we decided to turn back. It was a good thing we did because we met this park warden who stopped, talked to us quite a while and offered us some hot coffee.

"Later I decided to write and thank the warden even though I didn't know his name. I addressed the letter to Jasper National Park to 'The warden with a horse and a dog who was on the Skyline trail.' The Park Service figured out who that was and forwarded the letter to Dave. He wrote back and we decided to meet for a

69

date. Shortly after that we got married and Dave retired from the Park Service. We lived in Jasper for five years where Dave worked as a carpenter and I taught. Then last year we moved up here to Hinton. Three years ago we took the Willmore trip as a holiday and then last year we started working for Dave Manzer as wranglers," Anna concluded.

We rode into Blue Grouse Camp late in the evening. The camp set a few hundred yards back into the forest from a broad meadow. A roaring, sparkling stream tumbled down the mountainside right next to our tent. It started raining hard as we arrived so Wendy asked me if I would unsaddle Emily and Jessica's horses. Little did she know I had never saddled or unsaddled a horse in my life—more adventure. After undoing the cinch, breast strap and crouper, I slid the saddle off. Do you remember seeing the cowpokes in the western movies sling their saddle over their shoulder and mosey over to the saddle rack? It doesn't really work that way. I had a hard time lifting the saddle—no chance of slinging it over my shoulder. I did get it to the saddle rack without dropping it in the mud.

Dave M wanted to get all the horses in the corral so they could be fed before turning them out to pasture. He asked me to would open and close the corral gate as the wranglers unpacked the horses and brought them down. He said I could keep all the tolls and tips. I opened and closed the gate twelve times and never collected a dime—cheap crowd.

"Grandpa! Come see the rainbow," Jessica called from the edge of camp as I closed the gate the last time. Running down to where she stood I saw a brilliant double rainbow stretching completely across the sky, springing out of the roaring stream on the left, arching across the sky and diving into the cabin on the other side of the river. The rainbow framed the snow-covered mountain with the kelly-green forest below. The sight of it took my breath away.

Emily and Jessica ran up to play in the mountain stream. They launched leaves and sticks and then tried to bombard them with rocks as they floated down.

"Can we take our boots off and wade?" Emily asked.

"Sure."

The fact that the stream began as melted snow and never warmed up above 36 degrees didn't phase them. They waded across, hopped out on the other side and then waded back. As they played in the water, I cut some willow sticks for them to roast marshmallows on. When they finally got cold, we all went down by the campfire to warm up and roast marshmallows. Marilyn's marshmallow bag must have held a thousand marshmallows and that was a good thing because the girls roasted them once or twice a day every day of the trip. The cook also needed marshmallows for dessert and hot chocolate.

Dave M grilled huge, tender pork chops over the campfire for supper. Everyone, including Emily and Jessica, went back for a second one. Boiled potatoes with parsley, applesauce and a crisp cabbage salad rounded out supper. Marilyn sprinkled crunchy, dry Chinese soup noodles over the salad. They tasted better than croutons, another delightful meal. We were definitely living high on the hog!

I could hear sounds of the mountain stream gurgling down the hill beside our tent, the gentle wind through the trees overhead and the horse's bells tinkling in the distance as I lay in bed at night. It doesn't take long to fall asleep with such peaceful, natural sounds.

Chapter 9

The Night the Wolves Attacked Grandpa

"Get out of the oats, mule," I heard Dave Carnell yell in the middle of the night. Jack mule had uncovered the feed sacks stored under a tarp by the cook tent and broken open a sack of oats. Dave closed the sack, pulled the tarp over the bags and put a couple of logs on top to keep the horses/mules out.

I got up at dawn and went to the cook tent for a cup of tea. Dave C and Marilyn had the fire going in the cook stove and I slid up close to it to warm up.

"When did your family come to Alberta?" I asked Dave.

"Three or four generations ago," Dave said. "My grandfather used to deliver mail on horseback down around Mountain View a hundred years ago. He told me about one winter when the snow was really deep. He rode back in the hills to deliver the mail with three feet of snow on the ground and more coming down. Grandpa said he got into a deep snowdrift and the old plug horse the Post Office furnished just gave out, lay down and died. Grandpa was about 30 miles from town and couldn't walk out through the deep snow so he slit the horse's belly open, scraped out the innards and climbed inside the warm carcass to keep from freezing to death.

"During the night a pack of wolves appeared and started taking bites out of the dead horse. Grandpa said he was sure they would eat him after they finished the horse so he yelled and startled the wolves. Then he reached out and grabbed the tails of two of the biggest wolves. The wolves yelped and started running down the trail dragging grandpa and the horse. Grandpa said he held onto their tails until they got back near town. Then he let go of the wolves and walked home. He told me he'd have frozen to death if it wasn't for them wolves."

"That kind'a sounds like a tall tale," I said.

Dave grew up in the National Park and spent most of his life there

"I thought so too," Dave said, "but after grandpa died one of his old friends gave me one of the cancelled letters grandpa was carrying that day, so I guess it's true."

"How did you end up being a park warden?" I asked.

"My dad was a carpenter for the Park Service so I grew up in the national park," Dave said. "All of my boyhood heroes were park wardens. When I got old enough to work, I got a job on the trail crew in Waterton Park, Alberta. In 1973 I moved to Jasper National Park and became a park warden in the Brazeau District, covering about 500 square miles. I'd take a packhorse and make a two-week circuit of the backcountry, checking the trails, campsites and cabins. I loved being out in the woods by myself."

"How did you meet Anna?"

"That was pure, dumb luck. I was out one or two days from the trail head checking the trails on a cold, windy, rainy day when I came upon these two women hikers. They were soaking wet, cold and miserable so I stopped to talk to them. Anna was pretty shy and quiet. She let the other lady do most of the talking. The lady asked about the trail and the weather forecast. I could see they didn't have enough warm, dry gear to hike comfortably so I recommended they head back to the trail head."

"About a week later I got a letter from Anna thanking me for my advice and help. I wrote back and then we started talking on the telephone. Soon after that we met, started dating and then got married. That was about when I retired from the park service. We lived in Jasper and I worked as a carpenter. Last winter we moved up here to Hinton. I met Dave Manzer at the Eagle's Nest Camp awhile back and he called last year and asked if I'd like to work for him. Anna and I did a few trips last year, but this is our first full summer of wrangling for him."

After breakfast, Emily wanted to brush and feed her horse, Pepper.

"I'd like to take Pepper home," Emily said. "We could build a corral in the backyard. Chris wouldn't have to mow our grass anymore, Pepper could eat it."

"What about Sky (Emily's Siberian Husky who lives in her backyard)?" I asked.

"Sky likes horses," Emily said. "They would get along fine."

"Do you ride a lot back in England?" I asked Hannah as she fed the horses.

"Oh yes," Hannah replied. "If I'm not riding show ponies I'm riding on fox hunts."

"Isn't that a pretty expensive hobby?" I asked.

"I'm not chasing the fox, I'm taking care of the horses for the people who are on the chase," Hannah explained. "The hunt is an all-day affair. I help saddle the horses before the ride, hold the horses when they stop for lunch or tea and put them away at the end of the hunt. The forests we ride through have wide, deep drainage ditches and often one or two horses and riders will fall into the ditch. Then we get three Irish Cobbs and pull the horses out."

"Is an Irish Cobb a big guy or what?" I asked.

"No, they are very strong Irish draught horses," Hannah explained with a laugh. "We get very good tips for recovering the horses from the ditches."

Late in the morning we mounted up and every one except Hannah and Anna rode up to Blue Grouse Pass. We followed the stream through the thick forest with Wendy riding in front of Emily and Jessica and me behind. As Wendy would explain something about the trail or the sights, the twins started replying *"Whaaat evahhh,"* mimicking the catch phrase the society girls used in the 1997 movie "Clueless." Emily's 16-year-old sister, Kelsey, saw the movie and uses "Whaaat evahhh," occasionally at home.

"I saw that movie," 17-year-old Andy said. "I used to say that around the house until my dad got tired of it and forbid me to ever say it again. I almost forgot about whaaat evahhh, it's been so long," she said with a laugh.

"And you girls can forget about it too," Wendy said to Emily and Jessica.

We dismounted just above the tree line for a rest. Suddenly the thumping sound of a helicopter rotor shattered the mountain stillness. A Park Service helicopter materialized out of the trees, flew up the valley below us and disappeared around the mountain. A little later it came back down and flew toward the trail head.

"I always dreamed of flying helicopters for the Park Service," Dave C said. "After I retired as a park warden, I went to flight school and learned to fly helicopters. I've got 105 hours in them. After I got out of school, I applied to the Park Service and every company in Alberta for a flying job. The only jobs available were high-risk pipeline or oil rig jobs with a fly-by-night company known for not paying their bills. I'd still like to do it if a job opened up with the Park Service."

We climbed to the top of the mountain for a better view

"Let's roll down the hill," Wendy suggested to Emily and Jessica.

"Yeah!" the girls agreed.

Two-foot high willow bushes covered the hillside. Wendy turned a somersault in the willows and disappeared down the hill with Avery barking after her. Emily and Jessica followed, rolling ass over apple cart down and down and down, laughing all the way. Then they climbed back up the hill and started rolling down again. After rolling down four times, they climbed back up and fell asleep, Jessica laying in the willows and Emily with her head in Dave C's lap.

We rode on up to Blue Grouse Pass and ate lunch. Dave C lay back after lunch and took a nap. After he'd fallen asleep, Wendy put a piece of her sandwich on Dave's chest and motioned for Avery to go get it. Avery obeyed and licked Dave's face in the process of eating the sandwich. Dave opened one eye, looked at Avery, pulled

We saw 20 mountain goats from Blue Grouse Pass

his hat down over his eyes and went back to sleep. It takes a lot to disturb Dave.

"Can we climb the hill, grandpa?" Emily asked.

"Sure," I agreed. She and I started up the steep, rock-strewn hillside. We climbed up and up and up, pausing 1,000 feet above our lunch site to rest and then climbing up to a snowfield. Emily started climbing in the snow and sliding down while Avery chased her up and down the snowfield. Then Emily threw snowballs and Avery jumped in the air to catch them.

"There's a bunch of mountain goats," I said, pointing to the mountain across from us.

"Those little white things are mountain goats?" Emily asked.

"Yeah. There must be 15 or 20 of them over there," I said.

We watched as the herd moved up the mountainside, stopping periodically to graze.

"There's one there," Emily yelled excitedly, pointing down the hill to our left. A big mountain goat stood 100-foot away staring at us while another walked up alongside it and stopped. As I stood up, both goats walked leisurely off to the left, out of sight.

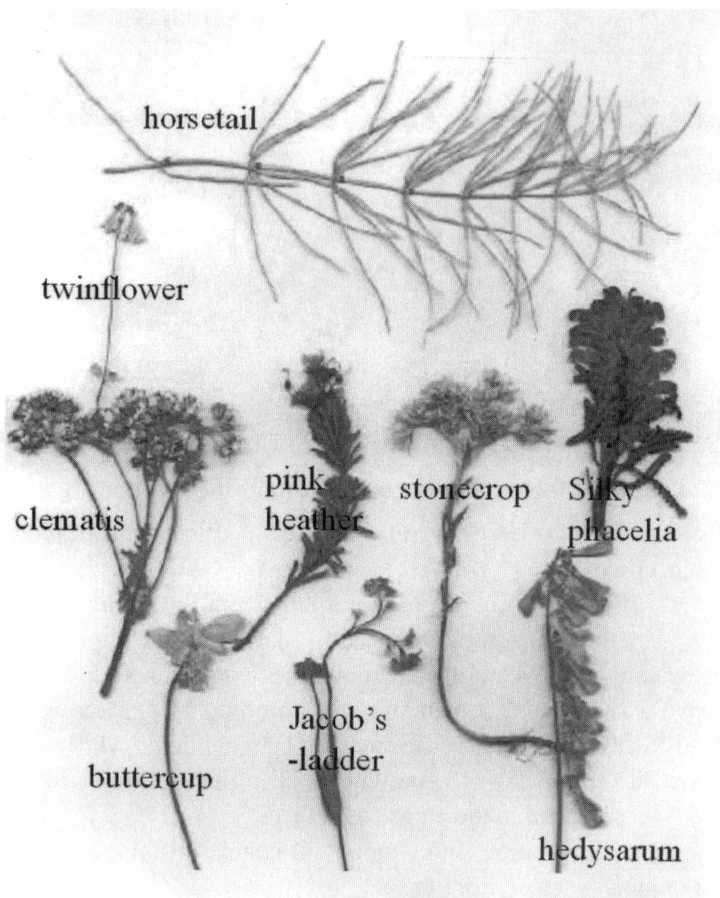

Some of the dried flowers the girls collected

While Emily played in the snow, I started following the goats to see where they went. I walked a couple of hundred yards around the mountain looking for them, but never caught sight of them. Florence, who was down the hill, told me later that she watched five goats climb the hill toward us and when I started around

78

Jessica and Wendy trying out their whoopee rodeo pose

after them, they kept moving, staying just out of sight in front of me.

Walking back to get Emily, I picked up dozens of broken geodes filled with sparkly crystals from the rocks on the side of the hill. When I got back, Emily and I climbed back down the hill to the horses. Florence decided to hike back to camp with Ray while the rest of us mounted up and followed a different trail back.

"See the claw marks on the spruce trees?" Dave M asked. "The black bears scratch the trees and then come back later and lick the sweet sap that oozes out."

"What's this funny weed?" I asked, pointing to a six-inch high, leafless plant with dozens of thin branches growing from the shoot."

"That's called 'horsetail'," Dave M said. "It is a very primitive plant. They find it fossilized in 60-million year old sediment. It was one of the first plants to appear up here and it is still around."

"Can we trot?" Jessica asked Wendy.

"Sure," Wendy agreed. Off the three of them trotted with their right hand punching the sky and yelling "yippee ki yey." We may have two future rodeo riders on our hands.

Back to camp, Emily and Jessica wandered off into the forest looking for bones.

"If you get lost, just head for the sun and you'll run into the mountain stream," I told them. "Follow the stream back uphill and you'll find the camp."

"We can find our way back," Emily assured me.

The girls came back to camp three times to get me to come see their discovery. I followed them several hundred yards back into the forest to where they found bones. Each time we would speculate on what kind of animal the bones belonged to and how it died. The girls never got lost and could always lead me right to the next set of bones. They were fearless.

When they finally tired of bone hunting, we walked down to the mountain stream. Anna told us that she had soaked her feet in the stream and how good it felt. The temperature of the water was about 36 degrees. Emily, Jessica and I took our boots off and soaked our feet. After about five seconds in the rushing water, my feet turned a bright pink and I lost all feeling. I had to rub them to get the circulation going again and then repeated the cycle. It felt refreshing, especially once my feet stopped hurting.

We planned to camp at Blue Grouse for five days and were almost out of firewood so Dave M and Dave C took the chainsaw up the hill and cut down four 50-foot tall dead spruce trees. They sawed the branches off and then hooked Eeyore up to a logging chain and skidded the logs down to camp one at a time. Emily, Jessica and I watched from a safe distance as Dave C used long reins to steer Eeyore and snake the logs through the thickly forested hillside. I felt like I was in an old-time logging camp watching the

The stream was cold, but refreshing

lumberjacks at work. Dave and Eeyore were poetry in motion as they brought those 500-pound logs down the hill and up into camp. Once all four trees were in camp, Dave cut them into one-foot lengths with the chain saw. Wendy and Mark chopped the logs into kindling for the cook stove and campfire. Mark split the 12-inch diameter logs by burying the axe head in the log with the first mighty swing, raising the log over his head and bring the axe and log down onto another log. The axe head hit the other log and the log's weight drove the axe deep, splitting the top log. Once the log was split in two, Mark would split off kindling-sized sticks with a single swing of the axe. Mark and Wendy worked until supper, splitting a nice-sized pile of kindling.

Marilyn served us creamed chicken with mushrooms over steamed pasta noodles for supper and a five-bean salad. In the seven days we'd been in the woods we've had a different kind of salad every night.

After supper we all sat around the fire and listened to Dave play his guitar. Eeyore came up to the campfire. He liked Dave's

Emily, Jessica and Happy on patient Eeyore's back

music. Wendy helped Emily and Jessica stand on Eeyore's back.
Marilyn's dog, Happy, didn't want to be left out so she jumped up
on Eeyore's back. Eeyore just stood there looking wise and let the
kids play on his back.

Chapter 10

My Birthday Suit Doesn't Fit Any More

"Tinkle, tinkle, tinkle," a horse bell woke me at dawn. I looked outside and found Eeyore grazing next to our tent. Eeyore is a beautiful Fjord, a breed originating in Norway. He is shorter than American horses and stouter. His coat is a beautiful golden color with a contrasting coal-black mane. He is a very gentle horse now, but Dave M told me he acted quite wild 20-years ago when he first got him.

"Instead of following the switchbacks down the side of the mountain," Dave said, "Eeyore would leap off a cliff with a full pack and crash right through the trees, cutting corners to intercept the trail below. Once Eeyore decided to go straight across the muskeg bog instead of following the trail around it. He got to the middle and sunk down to his belly. He couldn't move and looked very embarrassed. I had to tie ropes to two horses to pull him out."

As I walked to the cook tent, I met Wendy brushing and feeding the two pinto horses, Abelard and Heloise.

"You seem partial to those pintos," I said.

"My dad gave me these horses for my birthday," Wendy said.

"Are they twins?" I asked.

"No, just brother and sister. Abelard is a year older than Heloise."

"Abelard and Heloise seem like unusual names for horses," I said.

"The names come from French lovers who lived back in the 1100s," Wendy explained. "Abelard founded a school of rhetoric in Paris. Heloise lived near the school with her uncle and Abelard often saw her working in her garden as he walked to his school. He fell in love with her and started writing letters to her. At Heloise's urging, her uncle asked Abelard to teach his niece rhetoric. Abelard seized the opportunity and under the pretense of study, made love to Heloise. Her uncle eventually found out what was going on and forbid Abelard from ever seeing Heloise again. At that point, Abelard and Heloise ran off to live together in the country. Heloise bore a son. They married, but Abelard kept their marriage secret to protect his reputation. Her uncle was so mad he hired some ruffians to beat up Abelard. While he recovered in the hospital, her uncle convinced Heloise to enter a convent. She didn't hear from Abelard for 12 years. Then she started writing him beautiful love letters and he wrote back. They never saw each other again, just corresponded.

Heloise remained in a convent long after Abelard died. They are buried next to each other in the Paris National Cemetery. Their true love story is as famous as Shakespeare's Romeo and Juliet."

"Odd, I've never heard of them before," I said. (As coincidence often happens, a month later I happened to be reading Mark Twain's "The Innocents Abroad" and when he toured Paris, he devoted a whole chapter of the book to the famous love story of Abelard and Heloise. Then, a week later I attended a musical play in Dayton called "Fame" and one of the aspiring actresses kept wishing she could play a love scene like Abelard and Heloise. The Good Lord has a funny way of tying all these things together.)

Marilyn cooked cheese pancakes for breakfast. We covered them with sour cream and applesauce—dddddelicious!

"The air up here is so clean and fresh," I said to Dave M as we drank our tea after breakfast.

"Funny you should mention that," Dave said. "A fellow comes up from Los Angeles every year and I bring him out here. He carries along half-a-dozen vacuum bottles. We ride up in the mountains and he opens those bottles, takes samples of the air and seals them back up. He said the Willmore air is the cleanest in the world and they use his samples as a benchmark to measure air quality against."

Anna set out the fixings for our lunches: peanut butter, jam, bagels, tortilla shells, cream cheese, cheddar cheese, creamed chicken, bean salad, carrots, lettuce, cucumbers, oranges, apples, plums and candy bars.

Mid-morning we climbed into the saddle and headed for Marie Lake and Brewster's Wall. Wendy thought Emily and Jessica needed some more adventure so they each rode Eeyore half-a-day. Jessica started off on Eeyore and Emily rode Pepper.

As we rode through the scrub willow bushes, I noticed a lot of tall-stemmed plants with beautiful deep blue flowers, called monkshood. I picked a blossom and saw an intricate hood and petals protecting the delicate stamen.

"Horses don't eat them because they're poisonous," Wendy said.

"How do they know what's good and what's bad for them?" I asked.

"It's called horse sense," Wendy said with a laugh.

Happy scared up a snowshoe hare on the trail. The long-legged, brown hare bounded down the trail and then off into the brush with Happy barking behind. She never caught it. The hare turns a camouflaging white in the winter.

I pointed out a beautiful, multicolored butterfly to Wendy.

"We have some very exotic butterflies in Alberta," Wendy said. "A few years ago one of our park wardens was in Europe and he attended an art show. He noticed mounted butterfly collections for sale and realized that a number of the prettiest butterflies were endangered ones from Alberta. He reported his suspicions to the Canadian FBI (Federal Butterfly Investigators) and they apprehended a gang of thieves trapping and selling these endangered butterflies for up to $25 each. They went to trial, but got off scot-free because butterflies aren't on the protected list in Canadian National Parks. The rocks are protected, the animals, the birds and the plants, but the insects weren't. So they passed a new law that protects all living things in our parks, even the mosquitoes.

A beautiful butterfly landed on Emily's hand

"Under the new law, if a mosquito bites you, you can be fined for feeding the wild life. If you brush a mosquito away, you're liable for harassing the wildlife and if you swat it they can arrest you for poaching," Wendy said.

In fact, the mosquitoes didn't seem to be a problem in Willmore. Occasionally a few would land on me or appear in the tent, but not many. Even though the twins are identical, Jessica seemed to be a mosquito magnet and Emily a repeller. Jessica had four or five bites on her head and neck while Emily had none.

From the top of a low pass we caught sight of Marie Lake, an azure-blue lake nestled up by a sheer wall of stone.

"How did Marie Lake get its name?" I asked Dave M.

"One of the original outfitters in this area 100 years ago was named Fred Brewster," Dave said. "His wife's name was Marie and Fred named the lake after her. That sheer rock wall is called 'Brewster's Wall' after Fred."

We stopped at a camp on the shore of Marie Lake and ate lunch.

The girls went swimming in their birthday suits

"You girls want to go swimming in the lake in your birthday suits?" Wendy asked Emily and Jessica.

"Mine doesn't fit any more," Jessica replied.

"Grandpa didn't put it on the clothes list for the trip so I didn't bring mine," Emily said.

"What were you wearing when you were born?" Wendy asked, trying to rephrase the question.

"I wasn't very old then. I don't remember," Jessica replied.

"Think about it!" Wendy said. "Nothing! That's your birthday suit."

"Oh," said Emily and Jessica simultaneously. "Okay."

The men stayed in camp while the women walked down to the lake for their dip. Florence went along as the official photographer.

"Did you get photos of them swimming?" I asked Florence when she returned.

"Yes, I snapped a few shots of the girls bashfully covering strategic parts of their 'birthday suits' with towels and a distant shot from the back as they waded into the cold water. Emily and

Florence is a strong hiker & outstanding photographer

Jessica splashed around in the shallow water while Wendy ventured out neck deep into the lake. Then all three raced back to the shore, screaming and laughing, to dry off and get their warm clothes on."

"That's a beautiful camera you have. Do you work as a professional photographer?" I asked.

"No, I'm a nurse," Florence replied. "Photography is just a hobby."

"What kind of nursing do you do?"

"At present I'm not actively nursing," Florence said. "I handle the computers and website for the Alberta Nurse's Union. That job is a lot less stressful than nursing. I also help Dave Manzer with his communications. When he's out in the back country, I manage his e-mail inquiries."

On our ride back, 16 elk looked up curiously as we rode our horses out of the spruce forest into the meadow. The bulls watched us intensely as the does and fawns continued to graze. As we rode further into the meadow, the lead bull decided our presence posed a threat to his family so he signaled to the others that they

Florence is a nurse who runs the computers and website for the Alberta Nurse's Union

should move on. The graceful bulls held their heads high so their huge racks sloped backwards to avoid getting caught in the low hanging branches as the herd silently melted into the forest.

A little further along the trail, Dave C spotted some big horn sheep high up in the nearby mountain. Everyone stopped and Dave M let us look at them with his motion-stabilized binoculars. The lead ram had a huge set of horns that curved around to almost form a complete circle.

"That's a prize catch, there," Dave said as he studied the ram. "It now costs $22,000 U.S. per person for a ten-day big horn sheep hunt and there is no guarantee you'll bag even one sheep."

Emily switched to ride Eeyore in the afternoon and Jessica rode Pepper. As we passed through a thick part of the forest, the trail took a quick zig to the left to avoid fallen trees and dead branches, and then a zag back to the right to end up in line with the original trail. The four horses in front of Emily followed the first zig, but Eeyore decided to cut straight through the dead-branch tangle with Emily on his back. It sounded like an elephant crashing

We saw big horn sheep with trophy horns

through a jungle thicket as Eeyore bulldozed his way through the tangle, breaking off dead branches as he went. I rode immediately behind Emily and was sure she would be all scratched and cut up if she got through at all.

I trotted around the zig and zag to see where Emily and Eeyore emerged. There she sat, upright in her saddle without any visible injuries.

"Are you okay?" I yelled excitedly.

"Yeah, I'm okay, grandpa," Emily replied, "only I don't want to do that again."

We checked her over head to toe and miraculously, she didn't have a scratch on her.

"How did you get through without getting hurt?" I asked.

"I just lay back flat on Eeyore's hind end and closed my eyes," Emily said.

We climbed up on top of a high, razorback knoll well above the tree line. From the top we could see our camp, the river below, Blue Grouse Pass where we rode the day before, Glacier Pass 50 miles away, the big horn sheep we had located earlier, Marie Lake

It felt like we were riding at the top of the world

and Brewster's Wall—a breathtaking panorama. I was on the top of the world.

The ride down turned out to be breathtaking also, as much from the danger as the beauty. We rode down the mountainside into the thick spruce forest with no trail. The horses had to step over dead trees, across small streams and through tangles of small pine trees with no sign of an opening or game trail. Bushwhacking again! At one small stream, Lois' horse, Blue, jumped unexpectedly and Lois ended up out of the saddle and clinging to Blue's neck. Instead of screaming bloody murder, Lois calmly said, "Help." Hannah, who was riding right behind her, stopped all the horses and coached Lois back into the saddle. Blue actually raised his head and maneuvered himself around to help Lois get back on top of him. Dave M said we all earned our "Mountaineering 101" badges for that ride.

Once back in camp, Emily and I walked down the hill to visit the beaver dam. The beavers had built a three-foot high dam across one of the tributaries to the South Sulpher River. Their ten-foot diameter house stuck out of the water about five feet high. In the clear water we could see two underwater entrances/exits to the house. Inside, the beavers built up the floor to where it was above water level so they could sleep high and dry. The house was in good repair, but we didn't see the beavers.

Marilyn and Anna served shepherd's pie with macaroni salad for supper. I topped that off with hot pumpkin pie covered in Redi-Whip and a cup of tea. I probably gained ten pounds on the trip—the food tasted great!

Emily and Jessica roasted marshmallows over the campfire while Marilyn played popular tunes on her recorder. My favorite was "Loch Lomond." As I sat there with my eyes closed, my belly full of pumpkin pie and smelling the campfire smoke, Marilyn's recorder reminded me of Pan's magic flute.

Chapter 11

The 100-Yard Mosey

I packed crabmeat sandwiches for my lunch, using the crabmeat left over from the egg cakes with crabmeat breakfast menu. Each day was a culinary surprise as Marilyn dug deeper and deeper into the food boxes.

"Where did you learn to cook for a gaggle of people?" I asked Marilyn.

"Just cooking for my family," Marilyn said. "I raised four daughters. They're all out of the house now, so when Dave asked me to come along on these outings five years ago, I jumped at the chance."

"Where do you work the rest of the year?"

"I live in Nova Scotia and teach piano, voice, recorder, violin, kindermusik and Tai Chi," Marilyn said. Before that I worked in social research for the Nova Scotia government's planning department. I had one daughter when I earned my two sociology degrees a McGill University, and three more daughters when I did my music degree at Acadia. My three youngest daughters are performing musicians. I started working for Dave as trail cook during the summer after my kids grew up and left home."

"There's several harlequin ducks," Wendy said, pointing upstream as we rode along the West Sulphur River. "Those are the camouflaged females, not the colorful males. The males fly to Vancouver and lounge around on the beach while the females sit on the eggs. I always thought that was just typical male neglect, but the ranger told me there isn't enough food in the alpine meadows for all the ducks so the males fly away to let the females eat the local food."

We passed through three camps on the West Sulphur Trail. Three lady hikers occupied the first camp, the second remained empty and a single rider with three horses occupied the last one.

Marilyn (right) is a music teacher and excellent cook

Periodically we stopped along the trail to search for sheep or goats in the nearby mountains. Emily cupped her hands and put them up to her eyes like a pair of binoculars as she searched for animals. I tried that and it really helped. Obviously there was no magnification, but the hand tubes helped me focus on one small area at a time and remove all the annoying side clutter.

Dave M kept us on the southfacing slope while riding up the valley. He said that side tends to be drier because of the constant sunshine. The shady trails along the northfacing slopes tend to be wet, boggy and buggy.

The valley leading up to Hardscrabble Pass had five beautiful waterfalls splashing down from the snow-covered mountains. The trail changed from dirt to broken-up rock. One of the mountains in the valley is named "Gun Sight Mountain" because a sharp "V" in the mountain resembles a gun sight.

A chilly wind blew down off the snow pack and the occasional light rain caused all of us to untie our slickers from the saddle, put them on and button up. The higher we rode, the colder

We rode the edge of the drift to avoid the deep snow

it became so I put on my wool hat and gloves and pulled my hood up.

Patches of pink heather, white heather and white mountain aven grew along the rocky trail, struggling to survive in the alpine climate. In the lower altitudes, we passed yellow marsh marigolds, red and orange columbines and white bog orchids. Willmore has a diverse floral garden.

Approached the pass, we encountered a deep snowdrift blocking the narrow passage. Dave rode Blaze out onto the snow looking for a safe route. About halfway across, Blaze sank down to his belly in the snow. After thrashing around for a minute or two, Blaze found his footing and struggled across.

"Don't come this way," Dave warned. "Follow the edge of the snow pack around the wall and climb up on that ledge."

Following the edge of the snow, we climbed up on a rock ledge. At the end of the ledge, the horses had to step down about three feet to the rocks below. Dancer hesitated to make the big

My horse hesitated stepping down the three-foot ledge

step, but with a little encouragement from my heels in his ribs he jumped down.

From the top of the pass we looked down on Azure Lake in Jasper National Park and could see the Ancient Wall, the Natural Arch and Mt. Rajah 25 miles away. As I marveled at the magnificent snow-covered mountains in the distance, Hannah pointed out four caribou grazing near the lake. Emily, Jessica and I watched as they ate their way toward the lake and then trotted off down the valley.

Turning from the caribou, I noticed a shaggy animal running toward me over the rocks a few hundred feet away. I thought it was Happy, our bearded collie camp dog, but just then Happy walked up in front of me. I looked again and identified the animal as a hoary marmot. His brownish coat looked light gray because his fur was white-tipped. He kept coming closer, stopping, standing up two- or three-feet high on his hind legs, looking at us and then running closer until he was just 50 feet away. Then he sat on a rock and watched us. Usually marmots are shy and hide from people, but this one apparently hadn't seen people for awhile and wanted to

We could see Jasper National Park from Hardscrabble

know what we were doing there. We may have been the first visitors he'd seen this year.

While sitting there watching the marmot and enjoying the view, I noticed Wendy's tan, weathered cowboy hat had the Olympic symbol on the side.

"Why does your hat have the five Olympic rings on it?" I asked.

"I won it in the 1988 Olympics in Calgary," Wendy said.

"What event?"

"The 100-yard mosey," Wendy replied.

"The 100-yard what?"

"Mosey, you know, to saunter or to mosey along. I competed against 25 other cowboys and I had the slowest mosey for the 100 yards."

"I didn't know moseying was an Olympic event."

We looked down on beautiful Azure Lake

"Well, Calgary is a cow town and they included it in the 1988 Olympics. They have a bunch of strange Olympic events like precision swimming, race walking and skateboard jumping. In 1988 they included the mosey."

"Why can't you just walk in circles or stand there until you're the last person on the field?" I asked.

"Oh, no," Wendy said. "They have mosey rules just like race walking. It's very competitive. You have to keep some body parts moving all the time and keep making forward progress toward the finish line. They have judges with stopwatches on the field to make sure everyone is moving. They even use instant-playback from the TV cameras to settle disputed calls. About half of the contestants got disqualified because they got caught moving backwards or not making the required forward progress. If the judge sees you standing still, that's an immediate disqualification. Bumping into other contestants will get you a warning the first time, but you can be disqualified for interference. The hand position is also important. You have to keep at least one thumb tucked into

98

Wendy's Olympic winning "moseying" form

Avery sleeping on Emily, sleeping on Dave

your belt at all times. If the judge catches you with both thumbs showing at the same time, you're out of the race."

"Do you have to walk in a straight line?" I asked.

"Oh, no. The mosey can't be straight. You have to weave back and forth a little, but no part of the mosey can be perpendicular to the line between the start and finish, nor back toward the starting line."

"Did you have to practice before the event?"

"Oh, sure. I've been moseying all my life, but not competitively. When I decided to enter the Olympics, I started moseying six to eight hours a day, five days a week. The week before the event I was moseying all day long just to perfect my technique."

"Have you thought of going on the moseying rodeo circuit as a living?"

"No. I proved what I set out to prove in Calgary. I'm the best moseier in the world and I have the hat to prove it," Wendy said, pulling her hat down to shade her eyes from the sun.

"Could you show us your mosey form?" I asked.

"Sure," Wendy agreed, demonstrating her winning moseying technique.

Ray decided to hike back to camp from the valley below the pass so his horse, Redwood, ran loose and followed along with the riders up Hardscrabble Pass. That worked fine going up, but when we started back down Hardscrabble, Redwood decided he knew the way home and took off for camp by himself, disappearing down the trail. While the rest of us walked our horses down the rocky trail, Dave galloped after the runaway horse. He caught up with Redwood about five miles down the trail. A lone rider coming up the West Sulphur Trail saw the saddled, riderless horse trotting down the trail and stopped it. Dave caught up shortly after and recovered Redwood. Then he waited for us to catch up.

We rode into camp about 8:30 that evening after a long day on the trail. I felt tired, but not sore. A shorter ride might have been less tiring, but we took this trip seeking adventure, not rest.

The smell supper cooking greeted me as I walked passed the cook tent. I realized how hungry I was as I splashed water on my face and scrubbed my hands at the wash stand. After a delicious supper, we relaxed around the campfire and listened to Dave play his guitar. Emily and Jessica sang along as Dave played their favorite songs.

Chapter 12

The Baby Dinosaur at Fritzi Lakes

Crack! Bang! Boom! The lightning flashed and the thunder roared about 3 a.m. lighting up the tent like daylight. Emily and Jessica sat upright and called out in unison, "Grandpa, can we come in your bed?"

"I don't think there's room, dear. Let's just hold hands." Jessica grabbed Emily's hand and Emily held onto my hand as the thunder continued to rumble around us. We talked about their horses; their dog, Sky, and their cat, Speedy, until the thunder stopped. Then they went back to sleep.

I took a hot shower in the morning—all the comforts of home. The water temperature measured about 100 degrees F, but the air temperature stood at 40 degrees F. I didn't need a bathrobe as I stepped out of the shower tent because I was completely covered in a cloud of steam!

Our wilderness breakfast consisted of eggs Benedict with a sprig of parsley for color and Black-Forest ham—pretty basic.

"How's your leg?" I asked Emily as she came in the cook tent for breakfast. The night before she complained that her right leg hurt behind the knee. I checked it and couldn't see anything but a small bruise so I put Thera-Gesic pain relieving cream on it.

"It's okay," Emily said. Kids heal fast.

"Where are we headed today?" I asked Dave M as we mounted up and rode out of camp.

"To the Three Fritzi Lakes," Dave replied.

While riding across a big meadow, Emily and Jessica spotted four different sets of moose antlers in the grass and a caribou antler by the stream. They wanted to stop and pick them up so they could take them home to show their mother. We didn't, I took photos of the antlers instead.

The girls wanted to take the antlers home to mama

At the end of the meadow, we encountered a bog and Dave's horse sunk down to its knees in the mud.

"Let's cut up through the forest," Dave M suggested. Wendy led the way. The forest at the edge of the bog was clogged with small willow and spruce trees, but no trail. Wendy bushwhacked slowly up the hill with a dozen horses and riders following.

"There's no trail, the willows are too thick and there are too many downed trees to continue this way," Wendy yelled back down the line. "Let's back up."

Easier said than done! Dancer and I were wedged between a couple of six-inch diameter spruce trees with dead branches and willows all around us. No possibility of turning around and it appeared impossible to back Dancer 100 feet down through the dense growth. With a lot of cussing, grunting, groaning, crashing and milling around, the riders and horses maneuvered back down to the bog.

It was windy and cold at the Fritzi Lakes

"We'll stay right along the edge of the willows," Dave said. The horses splashed and stumbled through 100 yards of muddy bog before Dave found an opening in the forest. Then the horses climbed up on firm ground and followed a game trail, which led up to a small lake. While passing the lake, we heard crashing, limbs breaking and banging like a herd of elephants running through a bamboo forest.

"Probably a moose," Dave said. "They're pretty clumsy."

As we reached the timberline, the trail became very rocky.

"Dave and I will stay here with the horses and you guys can hike up to the lakes," Dave M said.

I grabbed my water bottle and lunch and started walking. The icy gale blew down the valley so hard I had to put my jacket hood over my hat to keep it from blowing away. Anna pointed out a grouse and her four chicks as we hiked past some scrub willows. The mama grouse ran about ten feet to the right of the trail and stopped while the chicks hid to the left of the trail.

The stream between the lakes emerged from a 20-foot diameter round hole in the rock wall

"Can you see the grouse over there?" I asked Emily and Jessica, pointing in the general direction where the camouflaged hen sat in plain view. They hunted for several minutes and never saw her. Then the hen clucked and ran a little further off the trail to lead us away from her chicks.

"I see her now," Emily said.

Continuing around the lower Fritzi Lake, we came to the stream connecting the three lakes.

"Look at the beautiful waterfalls," Jessica said, pointing to a 20-foot diameter round hole where the stream emerged from the solid rock wall. A torrent of water poured out of the hole and cascaded down to the rocks below.

"It would be fun to kayak through that tunnel," I joked.

"Not!" Jessica disagreed.

"Look at all the fossils," Emily said excitedly as she picked up fossil after fossil from the streambed. Fossilized coral, fossilized spiral shells and fossilized plants lay everywhere. In five minutes Emily and Jessica collected 100 pounds of fossils and piled them together.

"We'll pick them up on the way back down," Jessica announced.

Crossing the twenty-foot wide, six-inch deep stream posed a problem. I didn't want Emily and Jessica to get their feet wet on the way up because we still had a lot of climbing to do and their feet would get cold by the time we reached the snow fields. Anna and Wendy wore waterproof boots so they each carried a girl across the stream. I jumped from rock to rock and made it across relatively dry.

The edges of the lakes were covered with a dozen varieties of alpine flowers: purple monkshoods, blue gentians, white marsh marigold, golden fleabane, blue forget-me-nots, wooly louse warts and purple moss campion.

As we passed a rock ledge, Hannah stopped to answer the call of nature.

"I found a baby dinosaur," she yelled. "Come look."

We walked back to the ledge and there in the rocks were formations that looked like a 12-inch long spine, neck bones, a tail, a jaw and ribs. We took photos of Hannah's baby dinosaur and then hiked on by the middle Fritzi Lake.

"There are big horn sheep up on top of the ridge," Florence said, pointing to a 1,000-foot high ridge to the left of the lake.

I looked up and saw the five sheep silhouetted against the blue sky. By the time I got my camera out ten sheep stood on the edge of the cliff—then five more appeared and finally a total of twenty sheep stood looking down at us. They looked like Indians planning an attack on our wagon trail. Twenty sheep walked along the edge of the cliff, across a snowfield and disappeared into a cave. One ram stood outside the cave and acted as sentry.

Twenty big horn sheep walked along the cliff above

"Let's climb that cliff and follow the ridge line up to where the sheep are," Wendy suggested, pointing to the sheer cliff along the waterfalls between the middle and upper lakes.

Wendy and Hannah each took a twin and coached them up the 20-foot high cliff, step by step. I followed puffing and wheezing. I blamed the 7,000-foot altitude for making me short of breath. Emily and Jessica leaped from rock to rock and scampered up the cliff with no sign of fatigue. When we got to the top, I lay down in the grass by the lake and took a nap. Emily and Jessica ran around looking for pretty rocks and flowers.

"Let's climb up where the sheep were," Hannah suggested.

"You'll enjoy coming down the scree slide," Wendy promised Emily.

The wind blowing over the ridge so hard we had to crawl on our hands and knees and hold onto the grass to keep from being blown over the cliff. Slowly we climbed up and up, finally reaching the cliff where we saw the sheep. By then they had moved on.

It snowed on us while we climbed around the third lake

Scree consists of broken, flat pieces of sedimentary rock. The scree slide sloped down at a 45- or 50-degree angle for 1,000 feet.

"It's like coming down a sand dune or a snow hill," Wendy said. "You take a big step, sink your heel in the scree and slide. Then step and slide, step and slide, step and slide. It's fun! If you fall, just sit on your bottom until you stop sliding, get up and step and slide again."

We started down and the girls had a blast. They never fell, just kept running and sliding all the way to the bottom.

"Let's do it again," Emily suggested.

"No!" Wendy said.

At the bottom of the hill, I saw eight big horn sheep about 100 feet away grazing in the rocks. I whistled to get their attention. The sheep looked up, I took a photo, and the sheep put their heads down and continued grazing completely oblivious to us.

I found a big rock with three perfectly round, golf ball-sized nodules sticking out. I tried to figure how to break the big rock and carry the nodules home, but couldn't. Next time I'll bring my rock hammer and a little nitroglycerin.

When we reached the stream, Wendy and Anna carried the girls back across. Then Emily and Jessica retrieved their fossil collection. They could only carry a few of the 100 pounds they collected back to their horses. Both Daves appeared impressed with the size and quality of fossils Emily and Jessica collected.

The way back to camp passed through a dense forest with a lot of downed trees. Occasionally, Wendy had to get off Abelard and move or chop dead trees to make a passable trail. As we passed through the bog, Dancer took a big leap to extract himself from the mud. Again, his aerobatic leap surprised me and I hung on for dear life.

We met two heavyset male hikers on the trail. They lived in Kentucky and came up every year to hike Jasper National Park as part of their weight-reduction program. They started hiking in Jasper three days before, hiked over Glacier Pass, up the West Sulphur River and planned to cross over Hardscrabble Pass to get back to Jasper.

Marilyn had a blazing fire going back in camp so I snuggled up close to it to warm my cold, weary bones. I could have gone to sleep right there by the fire---the heat felt sooooooo good.

Emily and Jessica took a hot shower before supper. They gave up on the idea of skinny dipping in their birthday suits every day to keep clean. The shower felt warmer and easier.

Grilled pork chops, yams baked with oranges and peanut-butter frosted banana cake for dessert. Life is tough in the wilderness, but we'll make do.

Wendy braided Emily and Jessica's hair after supper. The girls got an awful lot of attention from the staff. Emily reciprocated by braiding Wendy's hair. Then Jessica and I played Kings-in-the-Corners while Emily roasted marshmallows for everyone. I went to bed about 9 o'clock, but Emily and Jessica sat in the cook tent talking while the staff washed dishes.

Emily braided Wendy's hair after she fixed Emily's

Chapter 13

Lost in the Canadian Rocky Mountains

"Sssssssssssssssss," my air mattress hissed as I opened the valve and rolled it up. We planned to move camp today and the wranglers wanted to pack the tents early. I roused Emily and Jessica out of their warm bed to help pack.

"We're just staying overnight at Moonlight Camp," Dave M said. "Pack a one-day bag with your toothbrush and a change of clothes so we won't have to unload all the luggage tonight. That'll save time repacking tomorrow."

I helped Wendy take down the tents after breakfast, roll them up and pack them on the horses.

"There's a spectacular waterfall back in the woods," Dave told me. "Take the trail above the meadow and keep bearing right. A mile or so into the woods you'll be able to hear the falls. There's no trail down so you'll have to bushwhack to it by following the sound. It'll take us a couple of hours to pack up. If you're not back by the time we get packed, we'll bring your horses and meet you along the trail."

The morning mountain air was cool at 7,000-foot altitude, even in mid-July so the three of us wore our jackets and hats. From Dave's description, I assumed I was looking for a waterfall on a stream coming down the mountainside and running into the West Sulphur River (fatal assumption). We hiked up the trail and kept taking the right-hand fork every time the trail split. After 30 or 40 minutes we hadn't come to the mountain stream, but I could hear the water to our right.

"Let's leave the trail and head for the sound of the water," I suggested to Emily and Jessica. Leaving the trail, we started plowing through head-high meadow grass, thick forest and thickets of willows toward the sound.

"Wait up, grandpa," Jessica called, "I'm stuck in the willows."

I went back and helped her untangle her boot from a grabby willow branchs. A little further along, I saw the stream.

"Let's stop, get a drink and try to figure out exactly where we are," I said. The stream flowed from right to left. I expected it to be flowing the other way as it came down the mountain (that should have given me a clue, but I remained fixed on the mountain stream idea).

"Where is the waterfall, grandpa?" asked Emily.

"I don't know, probably upstream. Let's go that way."

We bulldozed our way through the thick willows along the stream. In a few minutes a beautiful waterfall appeared. A huge torrent of bright blue water cascaded over a 30-foot high rock wall. The spray from the falls floated up, generating a vivid rainbow. The one thing that confused me was how I missed the mountain stream as I led the twins through the forest. I figured the stream must have come from an underground spring and we crossed above it. Based on that (bad) assumption, we either had to climb back up the hill and retrace our circular route through the forest or cross the stream and head directly back to camp. I chose to cross the stream (bad choice).

I took off my boots and told Emily and Jessica to take off theirs. The stream turned out to be about a foot deep and ice cold with rounded rocks on the bottom. I took Emily's hand and we crossed the stream, slipping and sliding on the algae-covered rocks. While Emily dried her feet and put her boots back on, I crossed back over and then recrossed it holding Jessica's hand. We all dried our feet and put our boots back on.

"Are we lost, grandpa?" Emily asked as she, Jessica and I plowed through a dense willow thicket.

"No, we're not lost. I'm just not sure exactly where we are," I said. "Our camp should be right over the hill."

"I'm tired," Emily complained while climbing over downed trees and through willow thickets. About half way up the hill, she tripped on a branch and fell.

"I can't get up," she yelled. "I'm stuck."

She had fallen with her head down the hill and her feet tangled in willow branches. I hurried back, picked her up and set her back on the trail.

Continuing up the hill, we soon came to a well-used horse trail.

"Just a little ways down this trail and we'll be in camp," I predicted (wrong).

From the top of the hill, I saw a river below us. It didn't look familiar, but it had to be the river by our camp. Following the path up the river and over the first rise, I expected to see our camp and the park ranger's cabin across from it. All I saw were trees ahead of us. Everything appeared terribly wrong. The river didn't look familiar, the mountains didn't look familiar and the trail didn't look familiar.

"We are lost!" I admitted. "I don't know where we are or where the camp is."

"Am I ever going to see my mommy again?" Emily asked with tears in her eyes.

"Yes, dear. Dave will find us. He wouldn't leave us out here."

I decided to head back down the river to where it intersected with the other river. The junction of the two rivers would be a good place to wait for our rescue. At the junction, I hung my red coat on a high tree branch as a signal for anyone looking for us. While sitting and waiting, I noticed the mountain on the other side of the river. It rose at a steep angle and the tree line occurred about 1,000 feet up. If I could climb up there, I could see for miles in all directions and possibly find our camp. In addition, I would be able to see Emily and Jessica all the time I was climbing and they would be able to see me all the way up.

The mountain I climbed to see where we were

"I'm going to climb that mountain and see where we are," I told the girls. "You wait here while I'm gone. Don't move from this spot. You will be able to see me and I'll wave to you as I climb up. Okay?"

"Okay," Emily and Jessica agreed. "Can we get a drink from the river?"

"Yes, you can get a drink, but don't go into the river or anywhere. Just stay here and rest."

I took my boots off and crossed the river. Then I put my boots back on and started through the willow thicket and up the hill. I climbed for five minutes and then stopped, waved to the girls and rested. The mountain was covered with willows, juniper bushes and other sticky plants and vines. Climbing the steep hill and plowing through the grabby bushes proved to be more exhausting than I expected. The 7,000-foot altitude and my anxiety factor probably had something to do with the difficulty. About two-thirds

114

of the way up, I ran completely out of energy. I'd stop, wave and gasp for breath. My mouth was cotton-ball dry---not enough spit to even swallow. I started crawling up the hill on my hands and knees.

After 30 muscle-numbing minutes of climbing I finally reached the tree line, turned around and saw the park ranger's cabin to my right, just beyond the hill.

Eureka! We're found! I knew exactly where we were and where the camp was. I could see the camp pasture just a mile upstream. I waved at the girls and started running down the mountain, grabbing branches and plants to slow me down as I took ten-foot strides. Reaching the river, I decided to cross with my boots on. I'd bruised my feet on the river rocks during my previous barefoot crossings. I jumped in the foot-deep water, splashed across and ran to where Emily and Jessica waited patiently.

"I know where we are," I said. "We're not lost! The camp is just a mile up the river. The waterfall was on the West Sulphur River, not on a mountain stream."

Emily led Jessica and me up the trail toward the camp. After walking for about ten minutes, I saw Dave and the pack train on the other side of the river. I yelled, whistled and waved my red jacket. One of the wranglers waved back. Emily, Jessica and I continued up the path to the river crossing and met Wendy and Andy leading our three horses.

"Wait on that side and we'll bring your horses across," Wendy yelled.

When she got the horses on our side of the river, we climbed into the saddles and then recrossed the river to catch up with the pack train.

"Sorry I got lost and held you up," I told Dave M when I caught up with the back of the pack train.

"No problem," Dave said. "It took us longer to pack up than I expected and we were just leaving when I saw you waving

Jessica & Emily never complained about the long rides

your coat. I've never lost or left anyone in the woods. I would have found you if you were really lost."

In 60 years of hiking and camping in the woods, this was the first time I'd ever been really lost. The two hours that I thought I was lost turned out to be a very stressful time. My fixation on the mythical "mountain stream" caused me to ignore all of the other obvious clues that the waterfall was on the West Sulphur River. I knew Dave would find us eventually, but considered the possibility that Emily, Jessica and I might spend a night in the woods. We could start a fire by focusing the sun on some paper using my eyeglasses as a magnifying glass. Feeding the fire going all night would keep us warm as the temperature dropped below freezing. I also thought about making a bed of leaves and brush, and covering up with leaves to keep the chill off. I'm very thankful I didn't have to use my Air Force survival training that day in the Canadian Rocky

After eight hours in the saddle, even the flat terrain seemed like a challenge (*Jessica likes to experiment with MicroSoft's Picture-It Putty program*)

Mountains. Yes, with God's help, Emily would see her mommy again.

I moved up to the head of the pack train at it stopped at a river crossing. The trail had grown over and Anna couldn't see where to cross.

"Let's cross here," Dave M said as he bulled his way through a tangle of scrub willows. The Sulphur River broke into several small channels and one main channel there. Dancer leaped over one of the small channels and my hat flew off at the top of the arc. I continued on bareheaded, knowing Avery would retrieve my hat. A few minutes later, Wendy rode up alongside and handed it back to me. Avery is a well-trained and helpful dog.

Dave C, Anna and I rode in front of the train as we crossed the river where the South and West Sulphur Rivers converge. As we started up the hill beside the river, Hannah yelled to stop. Some of the loads had become loose and needed to be tightened. Dave C rode back to fix the packs. While sitting there, Skeeter, a pack mule, decided she would go around us and get in front. I rode up the hill through the trees and cut her off. I sat there with Dancer's nose pointed at Skeeter until Dave got the loads fixed and the pack train started up again.

As we headed up the trail, I saw three hikers ahead of us. They had camped right in the middle of the trail. The forest was pretty dense and I guess there wasn't a clearing for them to set up camp so they chose the trail. Bad idea. Thirty-four fully loaded packhorses bore down on them and their camp. I could see sleeping bags flying off into the bushes; mattresses soaring through in the air; and pots, pans, backpacks and canteens being tossed off the trail. We held the pack train up until the hikers cleared the trail and then proceeded past them as they stood in the bushes in their underwear.

"Have a nice day," Anna called to them as we passed.

At the bottom of the valley, we crossed the main Sulphur River and headed up the Jack Knife Pass trail. We passed a 100-year-old trapper's one-room log cabin, the walls rotted and falling in.

I saw some huge yellow flowers Dave M identified as arnica, lots of pink wild roses, orange and red columbines, and purple fleabane as we rode up to the pass. The trail became steeper and rockier about midway up to the pass. While crossing Zenda Creek, I could look back down the trail and see 33 horses coming up behind me—a beautiful sight. It amazed me how surefooted the horses were on the steep, rocky trail. I would have had trouble climbing the trail on the rounded river rocks and slippery flat sedimentary rocks, but the horses plodded up the trail with ease. The wranglers continued to holler at the horses to keep them in line and coax them on. The sound of the horseshoes clanging on the rocky trail and the

We passed a dilapidated 100-year-old trapper's cabin

wranglers yelling brought back more movie memories—and I was really here to experience it.

"The plant with the little white flowers is called Labrador Tea," Anna told me. "Trappers and hunters used to make tea from the leaves and it's very high in vitamin C."

"But it tastes like hell!" Dave M said. "Very bitter."

"Hold up," Andy yelled from the middle of the pack train "A couple of the horses have loose packs." Dave M rode back to fix the loads, leaving Anna and me in front. It took 15 or 20 minutes for Dave to repack the horses. Black Jack and Festus, two young mules, decided they didn't want to wait for everyone else so they started crashing through the underbrush at the side of the trail to get around us. Anna stayed on the trail to keep order there while I bushwhacked up the hill to head off Black Jack and Festus. I got in front of them and Dancer stared them down. Dancer and Black Jack stood head-to-head for ten minutes until Dave called out for us to start moving. Anna started up the trail and I cut back down the hill to join her. Black Jack and Festus followed me back to the trail and ended up leading the rest of the pack.

We reached Jack Knife Pass late afternoon. The narrow rocky trail broadened out into a mile-wide meadow. We had experienced some difficulty keeping the packhorses in line on the narrow, tree-lined trail, but it became impossible on the broad open meadow. Instead of one, neat 34-horse string we soon had 5, 6 or 7 horses abreast crossing the pass. Dave M, Dave C and Anna rode out on the fringe of the melee, cracking their whips and yelling at the horses to get back in line, with little compliance. It seemed like each of the 34 horses thought they should be leading the pack.

Right at the crest of the pass, Dave M yelled for us to stop so he could fix the load on Festus mule. Five of us spread out in front of the stopped train to keep them from moving. Silver, a saddle horse that wasn't carrying a pack, walked around the edge of the group and headed down the trail in the direction we would be going.

"Should I go after Silver?" Andy yelled to Dave M.

"No, she won't go far," replied Dave. Silver continued down the trail a quarter of a mile and then, as predicted, stopped to graze and wait for us to catch up.

Dave M and Wendy repacked Festus' load and were tightening up the last ropes when Festus showed off. He kicked, reared, bucked, and brayed and took off up the trail. Dave had his hand wrapped around the load rope and Festus dragged him about 20 feet across the rocky ground before he could get his hand out of the rope. Wendy held the lead rope and hung on for about 50 feet while Festus dragged her through the bushes and over the rocks, kicking up a cloud of dust as she went. Wendy finally let go and Festus ran another 100 yards bucking off his entire load. Then he stopped and casually started grazing.

Dave M lay on the ground holding his bad hand. He had lost part of a finger on that hand last winter in a blacksmithing accident and it still wasn't totally healed. Wendy sat in the bushes brushing the dirt and sticks off herself.

"Are you hurt?" Anna called out.

"I'm okay," Wendy replied. (She told me later it's bad form to admit you're hurt.)

"Dave," Dave M called out to Dave C, "get a short rope on Festus and dally him to your saddle horn so he can't move."

Dave rode over and got a rope on Festus, led him back to where most of the pack lay and dallied him up short. Dave M and Wendy collected the pack and reload Festus. When Festus started to move, Dave M would rap him on the nose with his fist and tell him to stand still. Festus seemed to understand that he was in big trouble and settled down.

After repacking Festus, the pack train started down the trail. Silver waited for us to catch up and then trotted back in line. Reaching the tree line, we came to a huge burn area. Thousands of dead trees stood like telephone poles while thousands more fell over, blocking the trail in hundreds of places. The new trail weaved in, out and over the downed trees. A lot of small pine or spruce trees sprung up between the burned out ones, the rebirth of the forest.

Once beyond the burn area, Anna turned off Jack Knife Pass Trail and led us up The Indian Trail toward Moonlight Camp. About a mile into the forest, we came to a fork in the trail. Anna had never ridden this trail before, so she yelled back to Dave M, "Which way?"

"Go right," came the answer from out of the forest in front of us. We hadn't expected anyone else to be on the trail in front of us so the anonymous reply shocked us. It turned out to be Ray and our other three companions who had left early to hike from Blue Grouse Camp to Moonlight Camp. After exchanging greetings with Ray, Florence, Mark and Lois, we continued up the trail to the right. Twenty or thirty minutes later, we rode into Moonlight Camp alongside Snow Creek. Emily and Jessica rode into camp as I

Dozens of fallen trees blocked the trail in the burn area

unpacked my saddlebags. They had stripped down to T-shirts because the weather had warmed up.

Since we only planned to stay at Moonlight Camp for 12 hours, the wranglers put up one tent for Emily, Jessica and I. Mark, Lois, Florence and Ray all had their own hiking tents and the staff planned to sleep under a tarp. Marilyn and Anna fixed supper over the campfire and we ate a hearty camp meal sitting on logs around the fire.

I felt dead tired after supper. We had hiked and been lost for four hours, and then we rode for seven hours with only one five–minute restroom stop. I still wasn't sore from riding, but felt tired enough to sleep on the rocks and not notice it that night.

Chapter 14

Dancer gets a New Shoe

"Sara and the Englishman spent a night in the woods on one of our trips last summer," Dave M commented as we ate hot oatmeal with brown sugar and toast for breakfast. "They went for a hike late one afternoon and got lost. We looked for them until dark and then gave up for the night. Sara and the Englishman built a fire and sat up all night. Sara was a talker and she about drove the quiet Englishman crazy with her constant babble. We found them early the next morning. I don't know if the Englishman was more relieved at being found or at getting away from Sara," Dave said with a laugh.

"You'd better look at Dancer's left rear shoe, Dave," Anna said. "As I rode into camp last night behind Allen, Dancer's shoe looked loose."

Dave M walked over to where Dancer stood eating his oats and lifted the horse's left hind foot.

"It's not loose, it's bent," Dave said. "I'm surprised Dancer could bend it that bad without pulling any nails out." One arm of the shoe bent down at almost a 90-degree angle.

Dave unpacked his blacksmith tools, threw some more wood on the fire and led Dancer into the center of camp. He put on his leather apron and gloves, and then lifted Dancer's left rear foot and put it between his legs. Dancer stood perfectly still, even though he wasn't tied to anything. I guess he knew Dave planned to fix that bothersome shoe.

Florence handed Dave a pry bar and pliers to get the shoe off. In a matter of seconds, Dave had pulled the nails and removed the shoe. He put Dancer's foot down and took the shoe to the campfire. While the shoe heated up on the red-hot coals, Dave poured a cup of coffee and sat down. Occasionally he fanned the coals with a cardboard fan. By the time he finished his coffee, the

Dave removed and straightened Dancer's bent shoe

shoe was red-hot. He then straightened the shoe and put it back in the fire to heat up again.

Dancer stood on three legs, patiently waiting for his shoe to be fixed. Sometimes he had his shoeless, left rear foot raised and sometimes he raised his right rear foot. Dancer had his rear to the fire and never tried to turn around, though occasionally he turned his head to check on Dave.

When the whole shoe turned red-hot, Dave took it out of the fire using a pair of tongs and straddled Dancer's leg again. Then he placed the red-hot shoe on Dancer's foot. A huge cloud of blue smoke billowed up as the shoe burned its imprint into Dancer's hoof. I expected to see Dancer rear up and run for the hills, but he stood absolutely still, not moving a muscle. Obviously, Dancer didn't feel any pain from the hot shoe on his foot.

After the smoke cleared, Dave removed the hot shoe, walked over to a bucket of water and dunked the shoe to cool it. The water sizzled, spattered and steamed.   Then Dave took the cold shoe back to the patient Dancer, straddled his leg again and began nailing the shoe in place. Again, I expected some reaction from Dancer, but he just stood still and let Dave work on him.

"Good as new," Dave said as he flattened out the head of the last horseshoe nail. Dancer put his foot down and stood on it to see how the repaired shoe felt. Satisfied, he walked over to the hitching tree and stood waiting to be tied up. (Instead of hitching posts, the outfitters have pounded dozens of old horseshoes into the trees around camp to tie their horses to.)

"Horses have a good memory," Wendy said as she tied Dancer to the tree. "One of the old-time outfitters in the Rockies, named Pete Lund, went blind at age 90. He didn't want to just sit in his cabin until he died so he packed up five of his favorite horses and headed out into the backcountry. His horses knew the trail and where the camps were so he just let them have their heads and they led him from camp to camp. The horses walked right up to the hitching tree and stood there waiting to be tied up. Pete would tie them up, unpack, build a fire, cook supper and spend the night. He made several two-week-long trips before he died."

I let the girls sleep late since we didn't plan to leave before noon. They got up about 9 o'clock, ate breakfast and then played with the gray jays. The blue-jay sized birds are known as "camp robbers" because they fly into camp and steal an unguarded sandwich or piece of cake. They are also called "whiskey-jack" derived from a Cree Indian aboriginal myth of a birdlike figure they called "Weesakejac." The Cree word has been anglicized to "whiskey-jack."

Emily and Jessica took pieces of bread, sprinkled them around the edge of camp and then sat down and waited. A minute later several gray jays appeared in the trees and then flew down to eat the bread. As the girls put the breadcrumbs closer and closer to themselves, the jays hopped closer and closer. Emily tried to get the gray jays to eat from her hand, but they stopped a few inches away and waited for the crumbs to be dropped to the ground. Jessica put some crumbs on top of her beaver hat on her head. The jays flew down from the trees, landed briefly on her head to snatch up a couple of crumbs and then flew back up in the trees.

While the wranglers packed the horses, Emily, Jessica and I read another chapter of the exciting story of Kaya and her Indian horse. In this chapter she and her horse got trapped in a forest fire and were led to safety by a mysterious, smoky image that appeared out of nowhere.

After finishing the chaper, the girls and I walked down to Snow Creek and floated sticks and pine cones down the fast-moving stream. The girls launched their sticks simultaneously and then ran along the bank watching to see whose stick got to the small waterfall first. With all the twisting and turning the stream took, the rocks, roots and snags, it turned out to be a difficult course for the sticks to navigate and the lead changed often.

We rode out of Moonlight Camp about noontime, following the North Berland Trail down the North Berland River basin. After crossing the river, Wendy led us up the Indian Trail over the shoulder of the Persimmon Range toward Persimmon Camp. The weather had turned very warm and most everyone rode in T-shirts or short sleeves. The trail passed through an ancient forest of big, old trees. The forest in Willmore is somewhat unique in that there has never been commercial timbering, commercial mining or major developments in the park. Many areas, such as the one we rode through on this day, show no signs of being burned in the last 1,000 years. Basically, the area hasn't been disturbed since the last glacier receded 9,000 years ago. As a result of the age of the forest, dead trees littered the trail. The trail didn't run straight for more than 100 feet before it zigged and zagged to get around a downed tree. Huge trees had recently fallen in several places along the trail. Wendy and Dave C got off their horses and chopped or used the chain saw to clear the trail. Because of the economy measures instituted by the park service, they no longer maintain the trails and it is up to the outfitters to clear them.

The temperature dropped before we got to the pass at about 7,000-foot altitude. The girls and I put on our jackets and hats as we rode above the tree line. Once out of the thick forest, the alpine flowers appeared in droves. Fields of red, yellow, purple and blue dotted the mountainside.

Our group rode into Persimmon Camp about 5 p.m. and found the four hikers already there. By the time we got the tents set up, Marilyn and Anna had supper ready: vegetable stew, pasta noodles, crisp cabbage salad with crunchy Chinese soup noodles on top and chocolate pudding cake for dessert. Today was Dave Carnell's birthday so Anna decorated the campgrounds with flags and balloons. We ate birthday cake and sang to Dave around the campfire.

Wendy took out two slingshots to show Emily and Jessica how to use them. She hit her thumb on the first try, but hit the distant tin-can target on the second try. Emily and Jessica each collected a can of small, round river-washed rocks from the nearby stream to use as ammunition and started shooting at the target. They grew more accurate with each try and both knocked the can off the post 13 times before they ran out of rocks.

Then Wendy showed Jessica how to twirl a lasso rope. The big rope that Wendy used was too heavy for Jessica so Wendy cut a small one from a climbing rope she had. After a few minutes of practice, Jessica could twirl the loop and throw it around an unsuspecting water bottle or post. Jessica twirled for an hour, catching the water bottle a dozen times and a passing wrangler once or twice.

Dave M played his guitar and sang some of Emily and Jessica's favorite songs. The song I liked best related the story about a boy who was ten-years-old and barefoot, and the fun things he did to pass the time of day. The lyrics ended suggesting you'll find peace of mind if you keep your attitude ten-years-old and barefoot.

"Where did you learn all these songs?" I asked Dave.

Emily and Jessica learned to shoot the slingshots

"I performed in nightclubs in my former life," Dave said with a chuckle.

"So how did you get to be an outfitter?"

"Bad luck and poor management," Dave said. "It just sort of happened. I started out as a guide for small hunting parties in the Canadian Rockies and it just sort of grew into this."

"Where did you grow up?"

"I was born and grew up in Nova Scotia. I went to college and graduated with a degree in criminology. After college I worked at a prison in Nova Scotia and quickly decided that wasn't for me. In 1967 I moved to Alberta, fell in love with the mountains and got a job working with prisoners about to be paroled. After awhile I went to work on a Federal program designed to help parolees find a job. Didn't like that job much because the parolees didn't really want a legitimate job, they already had a drug job waiting for them. I quit and got into the ski business in the early 1970s, managing a ski resort. About that same time, I started in the guiding and outfitting business in the summer and playing and singing country

128

Dave played the guitar and sang almost every night

music in the winter. By the mid-70s, I quit the ski business and started taking adventure parties out during the summer and hunting parties out during the winter. Because of all the horses involved, I learned blacksmithing in my spare time. Now I spend one third of the year taking groups out in the Willmore, another third blacksmithing and the rest of the time sailing my ocean-going sailboat around the Atlantic."

"Where do you keep your sailboat?"

"A friend lets me dock it at his slip in Chester Basin, Nova Scotia, a little south of Halifax," Dave said.

"It sounds like you enjoy your life."

"I have a great time, riding around the Rocky Mountains, cracking my whip to keep the mules in line, telling stories, singing songs and maybe telling a few lies," Dave concluded with a big grin on his face.

Marilyn, Anna and Lois played trios on their recorders and Anna also played the spoons. She had a special set of two spoons mounted facing each other on a block of wood. The three ladies

129

Emily & Jessica sang along after hearing a song once

made great music that evening playing *"Green Sleeves"* and *"Going to Scarborough Fair"* along with other favorites late into the night.

Chapter 15

Fishing in Persimmon Creek

A buck mule deer sauntered into camp about 6 a.m. as Anna, Wendy and I sat around the campfire drinking our morning tea. It stood no more than 30 feet from us, apparently waiting for an invitation to come up to the fire and have breakfast with us. It had a big rack still in velvet. When he realized we didn't pose a threat to him, the deer lowered its head and started grazing on the fresh green grass at the edge of camp. We continued talking as the deer looked up periodically, apparently to catch the drift of our conversation and then went back to eating grass. After about five minutes, it looked up as if to say good-bye and then walked slowly out of camp.

"I've seen that deer in this camp before," Wendy said. "It's almost a pet."

Patches of dark storm clouds filled the dawn sky in all directions. Every 30 minutes, like clockwork, a cloud drifted overhead and opened up, producing a deluge of cold rain and the rumble of thunder. It didn't look like a good day for a ride in the mountains.

Marilyn cooked French crepes for breakfast with homemade wild chokecherry syrup and cottage cheese. I went back for thirds. Everyone lingered in the cook tent talking and drinking coffee after breakfast because of the rain.

"I think we'll stay in camp today," Dave M said. "I don't like riding above the tree line on a stormy day because of the danger of lightning. Does anyone object?"

"No," everyone agreed. No sense in tempting fate by riding out in a lightning storm.

As I scurried back to my tent, I noticed one of our party headed for the outdoor privy with an umbrella and a satellite phone. That conjured up an odd scene: A wilderness setting, a log nailed

**The cook stove had a two-foot square cooking area, a
two-shelf oven and a five-gallon hot water container**

between two trees to form the seat for the outdoor privy and a
camper with their pants down around their knees trying to dial
(punch) a satellite phone with one hand and hold the umbrella with
the other. Meeting of the old and the new. While there was no
charge for the privy, a call on the Motorola phone cost $1.50 a
minute over the Iridium satellite.

"Do you want to go fishing when the rain stops?" I asked
Emily and Jessica.

"Yeah," they agreed.

Mid-afternoon the clouds parted, the sun peaked out and
the sky cleared. We grabbed the two telescoping fishing poles I
brought from home along with my tackle box and headed for
Persimmon Creek.

"We won't get lost again, will we grandpa?" Emily asked.

On our one rainy day, we sat in the cook tent and talked

"No, dear. We're just going across the meadow to the creek, not through the woods," I replied. "I learned my lesson. I'll take the map, compass, first aid kit, water, whistle and matches. We are prepared."

The ten-foot wide Persimmon Creek ran about six- to eight-inches deep and fast after the morning rain. I tied a small, brightly-colored lure with a silver spinner on one of the fishing lines, cast it out in the center of the creek and handed the pole to Emily. Then I did the same for Jessica, about 50 feet down the creek. We sat and talked and periodically Emily or Jessica would pull their line in and cast it out again. Once, Emily almost snagged a black and yellow butterfly as she cast her lure out. After about 15 minutes of inactivity, Emily leaned her pole against a willow branch and started playing in the water with a stick. She retrieved long pieces of algae growing on the bottom of the creek and started mixing them with mud to make mud and algae patties. Jessica joined Emily and they

133

The fishing was great in Persimmon Creek---only the catching was poor

soon had a bank full of mud pies. Periodically they would pull in their line and cast it out again. After 30 minutes, they tired of fishing and making mud pies, and asked if they could climb the creek bank.

The bank consisted of finely crushed black volcanic rocks forming unstable scree. As the girls tried to climb up the steep bank, they would take one step up and slide two steps backwards. By grabbing onto grass and roots, Jessica finally conquered the ten-foot high scree bank. Then she reached down and helped Emily up the bank. Once on top, the girls slid down and started back up again. After a few ascents and descents, their boots were filled with small rocks. I helped them get their boots off, empty the rocks out and get them back on. This time we stuffed their pant-legs down in their boots to try and keep the rocks out. That worked for a little while, but they soon came back to get their boots emptied again.

It seemed strange to see our head wrangler clowning

135

Between sessions of emptying boots, I walked along the creek searching for new flowers. One of the interesting flowers I found is called a globeflower. The one-inch diameter petals formed a perfectly concave parabola that focused the solar heat onto the reproductive parts of the flower. Having attracted the insects with their yellow color and sweet fragrance, the globeflower offered a bit of warmth, encouraging the bugs to linger longer. While they tramp about enjoying the warmth, they pick up more pollen and carry it from plant to plant, aiding fertilization. The five- or six-inch tall globeflower has a cone of green pistils in the center, surrounded by bright-orange stamens; a very pretty and efficient flower.

That evening turned into show time. I was surprised to see Wendy, our rugged head wrangler, who periodically wrestled a mule to the ground to get his attention, emerge from her tent dressed in black tights, a black knit top, wearing a fluffy purple and black cocktail dress and a broad-brimmed orange sun hat. Emily wore a pink tutu and had her hair up on top of her head in dread-locks with a colorful scarf around it. Jessica wore a short red cocktail dress and a dread-lock hairdo. Hannah was decked out in a pink cocktail dress. Where did all this finery come from?

"Hannah and I bought it at the Goodwill shop in Edmonton for these parties," Wendy explained.

The show consisted of daring horseback acrobatics on Eeyore's bareback. Wendy, Emily and Jessica took turns performing while Hannah held Eeyore. They demonstrated all kinds of acrobatic poses except handstands—quite a show.

"How long have you been working with horses?" I asked Hannah after the show.

"All my life," Hannah said. "I was born in Taunton, England, in 1981 and grew up in nearby West Huntspill. My mother wanted me to become a ballet dancer, but I showed more interest in horseback riding than dancing."

Hannah is an accomplished horsewoman from England

"I started riding at age four. I've always been interested in horses and the outdoors. While I was growing up, I worked at a lot of different summer jobs including shoveling coal as a fireman on a steam engine train. I also took care of the horses on fox hunts.

"After high school, I enrolled at the University of Edinburgh and earned a master's degree in Social Anthropology. Then I went to work for a man who raised show ponies. I train the ponies and the children who ride them. They have a weight and age restriction on the pony rider. I have to be less then 100 pounds and less than 25 years old to show the ponies. Right now, I weigh 96 pounds.

"How did you end up riding for Dave?" I asked.

"I wanted to see the mountains of western Canada so I got on the Internet and found Dave's website. I sent him e-mail and asked for a job. He said okay so I came over last year for the first time and came back again this year."

The special dessert for supper consisted of rice pudding covered with brown sugar, cinnamon and almond bits. Anna hid two whole almonds in the pudding, like the English used to do with a six pence in the Christmas pudding. Whoever found the whole almonds won a prize. Emily found the first almond and Jessica found the second. They each got a prize of colorful, decorative wash-off tattoos.

It started raining again as we headed to bed. I found it quite soothing to lay in my sleeping bag, warm and dry, listening to the rain pitter-pattering on the tent roof. I woke up several times during the night to the sound of distant thunder and hard rain. The girls never stirred. In the middle of the night, Wendy yelled at the horses to get out of the feed sacks that had been stacked near the campfire. Andy slept under a tarp by the campfire to guard the feed sacks, but she never woke up when the horses stepped over her to get to them.

Chapter 16

Playing in the Waterfall

Horse bells woke me up every hour, on the hour, all night as one horse after another paraded past my tent. They apparently were on their way to or from the oat sacks by the campfire. Wendy said as soon as she shooed one horse away from the oats, another horse appeared out of the dark. She felt outnumbered thirty-four to one.

I was the first one up so I started the tea water heating on the Coleman stove in the cook tent. Dave C came in soon after I put the kettle on and we talked about his days as a warden at Jasper National Park.

"The best part of my job was when I rode out with a packhorse and my dog on a week-long trip to check the campsites and trails," Dave said. "Most of the time I didn't meet more than half a dozen people all day.

Anna, Marilyn and Wendy came in the cook tent about the time Dave got the cook stove going. Anna and Marilyn started preparing cornmeal pancakes while Wendy related another of her adventures.

"Our last trip up here started on July First, Canada's birthday," Wendy said. "Because I'm so patriotic, I painted Canadian flags on the front hoofs of all the horses using red and white fingernail polish. It took me two mornings and one evening to get around to all the horses. They attracted a lot of attention when we met another pack train on the trail, but it only lasted for one day before the horses wore the fingernail polish off. I guess I should have etched the flag design in their hooves first with a deburring tool and then painted the depression to make it stay on longer."

Sunrise over the Persimmon Range Mountains provided a spectacular sight. Wispy white clouds clung to the mountain tops as the golden rays of the sun streamed through the notches in the mountains and then poured over the tops as the sun rose higher. The morning fog lying in the bright green valleys added the soft colors of a Rembrandt painting. Pinch me, I think I've died and gone to Heaven.

Dave C noticed that Ernie had a puncture on the back of his left rear foot so he put some salve on it, got out the medical kit and filled a syringe with antibiotic. While Hannah held Ernie, Dave stuck a *big* needle into Ernie's neck and squeezed the antibiotic in. Ernie didn't move a muscle during the entire operation.

"Horses don't have many nerve endings in their neck," Hannah explained. "And the neck is a safer place to give a shot than the rump because you're not as likely to get kicked when you're by the horse's neck as compared to his hind end."

One thing that amazed me was the horse's selective sensitivity. Many times while riding the trail behind another horse, I watched a single fly land on the horse's rump and instantly the horse directed its tail to pick off that particular fly. They can feel the microscopic weight of a fly through a quarter inch of horsehide, but don't seem to feel a five-inch long needle being buried in their neck. The Lord did a marvelous job when he designed the horse.

After taking our obligatory group photo, we saddled up and rode up into the Persimmon Basin. The day dawned cool and clear, but started to warm up mid-morning. The twins and I dressed with five layers of clothes and as the sun started to beat down on us, we stripped off our jackets, sweatshirts, sweaters and shirts to ride in just our T-shirts. The bowl-shaped basin blocked the wind and helped warm things up.

A huge wall of snow crowned the sharp ridge at the southern edge of the basin. The prevailing southerly winds piled more and more snow on the ridge all winter. It built up like the leading edge of a wave with the crest leaning 20 or 30 feet over the edge of the cliff. As the snow warms up in the summer, this unstable projection will eventually come crashing down in a mini avalanche, but there

Our whole group posed for a camp photo

would be no danger to riders since the trail ran far down from the cliff.

As we rode into the center of the basin, Dave M pointed out some big horn sheep grazing at the east end of the basin. Three rams with huge curved horns looked up as two teenage sheep, three ewes and a lamb continued to graze. Drawing closer, the herd started walking slowly toward some house-sized boulders and disappeared behind them. We stopped, dismounted and watched a hoary marmot run after them and disappear behind the rocks. I'm not sure if he wanted to play with the lamb or just wondered where everyone went.

We stretched out on a grassy knoll, ate our lunch and enjoyed the beautiful mountain view. Emily and Jessica started playing fetch the stick with Avery and then started chasing after him as Avery ran circles of ever-increasing diameters.

We stopped to explore the waterfall

I marveled at the patterns visible in the mountain strata. The motion of the earth's tectonic plates pushed up horizontal sedimentary layers from an ancient sea until those layers now stood vertical. As the soft sedimentary rock eroded, it formed a series of huge wave-like designs, each wave at least 500-feet tall. God's artwork defies imagination—pure unique beauty.

Another marmot came out of his hole about 100 yards away and stood up on his hind legs to get a better view of the humans, horses and dogs that invaded his territory. It watched us for several minutes and then lay down next to its hole. Finally it must have gotten bored watching us and disappeared down in the hole.

After a short nap, we mounted up and rode along the south edge of the basin past several 20-foot high waterfalls. Finally we stopped by a waterfall with a cave underneath. A ten-foot wide, six-inch deep snow-fed stream tumbled over the rim of the falls and

The girls collected rocks in the cave under the waterfall

crashed on the rocks below creating a beautiful rainbow. I sat in the dry cave and viewed the mountains through a curtain of crystal water beads.

Emily and Jessica took off their boots and waded in the ice cold stream above the falls. Wendy and Anna were the only ones brave enough to take a refreshing dip in the stream.

As I sat enjoying the sight and sound of the waterfall splashing on the rocks, two golden-mantled ground squirrels appeared and started eating the nearby flowers. They would bite the flower off near the ground and then sit up on their hind legs and eat the petals as they twirled the stem around. When all the petals were gone, they cut a new flower and started on it.

We followed Persimmon Creek back down the hill towards camp. In the basin, the creek appeared crystal clear. At the edge of the basin, a very muddy tributary joined the creek, turning the water a brown coffee color. Dave said there was a lot of erosion in the

Dave had his saddles handmade by Roy M. McCaughey

soft dirt up that particular valley. We saw bear, moose and caribou tracks in the mud along the creek.

"Where did you get your saddles?" I asked Dave M when we got back to camp.

"There's a fellow named Roy M. McCaughey over in Sherwood Park, Alberta, who made them," Dave said. "He's an old outfitter who developed hip problems and had to have both of his hips replaced. The doctor told him he would never be able to ride again. That didn't set well with R.M. so he decided to design his own saddle. The seat of a western saddle tends to be wide and it bends your legs out at the hips in an unnatural way. Also, the stirrup lays parallel to the horse and you have to use leg muscles to bend the stirrup out perpendicular to the horse's body. R.M. designed his saddle with a narrow seat to let his hips hang normally and with the stirrup 90 degrees to the horse. The result is a very comfortable saddle. The saddles cost more, about $3,000 each, but my guests are much more comfortable so it's worth it. R.M.

built all the saddles I have. He has a waiting list for his new saddles and even his old saddles sell at a premium."

"The saddles are definitely more comfortable," I said. "With all the riding we've done, I haven't been saddle sore at all."

Marilyn served stir-fried tofu and vegetable over rice for supper and Emily and Jessica went back for seconds thinking the tofu was chicken. The twins started the trip with a lot of food prejudices, but developed a healthy appetite and acceptance of things they have never tried before. Being outdoors all day and the absence of a refrigerator full of ice cream, pudding and cookies has helped.

Marilyn and Dave M played and sang around the campfire after supper while Emily roasted marshmallows. Anna made popcorn to round out another perfect day in the wilderness.

It must be getting close to the end of the trip. I'm running out of Band-Aids, my digital camera batteries are dead and I'm down to one pair of clean jeans and one clean shirt. Several of the men who use electric shavers complained that their shaver batteries were dead. Mark Lund brought a small, portable solar battery charger to charge batteries for his camera, hand-held Global Positioning System (GPS) navigating device and flashlight. Mark said it only worked marginally.

"I was barely able to get one days worth of pictures from a full day's charge on one set of AA batteries," Mark said. "And that only worked when we were in camp since the charger had to be in full sunlight and repositioned every couple of hours."

Speaking of electric shavers, I don't use one. I've always been a blade man myself, but for this extended trip in the wilderness I decided to grow a beard. I'm 68 years old and have never grown a beard. It's not that my wife objected, I just never thought about doing it. Well, that changed on this trip. My beard grew very slowly and the quarter-inch of stubble at the end of the trip appeared pretty pathetic compared to Mark Lund's full beard, Dave Manzer's handsomely trimmed beard or Dave Carnell's nicely shaped moustache. Florence took a photo of me with a beard. I let the

The author showing off his first-ever beard
146

beard grow for a few days after the trip to show my co-workers
what it looked like. The next day, I shaved it off.

Chapter 17

The Forest Fire

Sunrise in the Persimmon Ridge Mountains started with a faint yellow glow in the east. Then the golden rays of the early morning sun crept over the mountain and reflected off the western snow-covered peaks. The deep blue sky behind and soft green valleys sloping down to the creek came alive as the sun inched higher. The cool, clear mountain air and the fresh scent of the spruce trees smelled of adventure. It doesn't get much better than this.

Moving day! The staff got up early and started taking down the tent while Emily and Jessica were still dozing in their sleeping bags.

"We can just wrap the tent and sleeping bags up with the girls in them and tie them on the horses so they can sleep as we ride to Eagle's Nest Camp," Wendy suggested.

"Not!" Emily yelled, overhearing the discussion. They scampered out of bed and headed for the cook tent and a breakfast of bacon, eggs and homemade biscuits.

"My Band-Aid keeps coming off, grandpa," Jessica complained. She had slipped on the wet rocks by the creek, fallen and cut the palm of her hand near her thumb. I put a Band-Aid on it twice, but when she moved her hand, the Band-Aid came loose.

"I can fix that," Anna said. She put a clean Band-Aid on Jessica's cut and then wrapped silver duct tape completely around her hand to hold the Band-Aid on. It looked like Jessica had a silver artificial hand, but the Band-Aid stayed on all day.

The four hikers left for Eagle's Nest Camp right after breakfast while the wranglers started packing the equipment. Emily, Jessica and I read another chapter of Kaya and her horse and then walked to the creek to play. The girls brought the two slingshots and floated cans down the creek as targets. Surprisingly, they hit the moving cans pretty often. After they tired of that, they changed the rules and ran a race to see whose can could float the furthest and the fastest. Then the game evolved into sink the can. As the cans floated down the fast-moving stream, they threw rocks at them and tried to sink them. The girls had no trouble entertaining themselves. What one twin didn't think of, the other one did. They played in the creek until Wendy called us to saddle up. Then they took the cans back to camp and put them in the garbage.

Anna, Andy and I started out at the front as the pack train left Persimmon Camp.

"How did you get to be a wrangler at such a young age?" I asked Andy.

"My mom and dad met Dave years ago at a horse clinic. I grew up in Edson, Alberta, and have been riding by myself since I was three years old. I love horses and being out in the wilderness. Dave is my godfather and this is the seventh summer he's let me come along as a wrangler."

"What are your interests in high school," I asked.

"I'm into about everything. I play the guitar, piano, sing, write poetry and dance. I'm interested in art, music, history, snow boarding, basketball, soccer, cross-country running and I'm captain of the volleyball team. I'm also known as the 'toughest chick' in school because I can beat everyone else in arm wrestling"

"What do you plan to do after high school?"

"I'd like to go to college and study art, history and tourism. Then I'd like to start a travel business taking senior citizens or big families on tours overseas. I'd know enough about the art, music and history to be a good tour guide and know how to handle all the arrangements for transportation, tours and accommodations."

"That's a pretty ambitious goal. How did you end up with a name like Andy?"

"My folks were expecting a son and they planned to name him Anthony after my Italian grandfather. When they found out I was a girl, someone suggested that Anthony in Greek is Andonia so they named me Carmella Andonia Roberto, but I go by Andy."

Andy was the 'toughest chick' in her high school

The ride started smoothly, with no fights between the horses or undue jockeying for position by the mules. An hour later when we stopped to fix a loose pack on one of the mules, Black Jack and Skeeter got into a braying match, both trying to move to the head of the line. A couple of cracks of Anna's whip over their heads quieted them down and we got the pack train back on course without incident.

We passed several nice smooth sandy hillsides on the trail and Black Jack tried to lay down and roll in the soft sand at every one. It took two or three wranglers yelling, "Get up, Black Jack—don't roll," to keep him from rolling and knocking his 160-pound load off.

The three hikers we met a few days before camping in the middle of the trail, showed up at the South Berland River crossing. The grandfather, father and son again had their sleeping bags and all their gear right on the trail. They frantically pitched sleeping bags and gear into the bushes as our horses crossed the river and marched through their camp. I thought they would have learned from our previous encounter, but I guess there were so few people back that far in the wilderness that they didn't think lightning would strike twice in one week.

While riding through the forest, Marilyn's dog, Happy, scared up four grouse in different locations and a bunch of their chicks. Happy appeared satisfied to flush them. She didn't try to chase and catch them.

This day turned out to be the hottest one of the trip. There wasn't even the hint of a breeze in the forest. While crossing over the ridges we enjoyed a refreshing breeze, but it died out when we rode down into the forest.

Dave suggested stopping at Hay Summit Camp for lunch. Someone had carved a throne chair using the stump of a three-foot diameter pine tree. Emily and Jessica took turns sitting on the throne.

Emily, Jessica, Hannah, Dave M and I ate a leisurely lunch while Wendy and the other wranglers took the pack train and headed directly to Eagle's Nest Camp. The rest of us planned to take the scenic trail up along the mountain ridgeline.

Starting up the hill to the ridgeline, we saw huge clouds of white smoke billowing up to the southeast.

"I hope that's the Park Service's prescribed burn down on Rock Creek," Dave said. "Otherwise we may have a wildfire to deal with tonight." The rest of the afternoon I watched as the clouds of smoke built up and then died down again.

From the 7,400-foot-high ridges between the Persimmon and Berland Mountain Ranges, we could see a hundred miles in all directions. Row after row of barren mountain ridges and snow-covered peaks fanned out in all directions. How in the world did the early explorers find their way through this jumble of mountains 150 years ago? They had no maps and no GPS.

We rode the treeless crest between the Persimmon and Berland ranges

We caught up with Mark, Lois, Ray and Florence at the top of one of the ridges and stopped to chat.

"We saw a caribou and her calf in the draw when we first got up here," Lois said. "They weren't 50 feet away."

Riding on, Dave pointed out a line of vertical black rocks extending ten or fifteen feet into the air. They were each a foot thick and three or four feet wide. The whole collection of rocks extended 40 or 50 feet across the hill in a line. They would make a perfect wall for a cabin or fort. These black, vertical rock walls appeared several places along this and adjacent ridges.

"I don't know how they were formed," Dave said, "but they are quite common around here."

We stopped at a knoll overlooking Thoreau Creek and Dave pointed out an old camp down by the creek.

"Back in the winter of 1928, the Blue Diamond Coal Company had a steam engine brought up frozen Thoreau Creek on a sled pulled by a team of six mules. If you look down there between the creek and the forest, you can see what's left of that engine."

I took Dave's motion-stabilized binoculars, followed the creek up the valley and finally found the steam engine. "It looks like most of it is still there," I said.

"Yeah, it's rusty, but still pretty much as they left it in 1928," Dave said. "They used the steam engine to power the drill for some exploratory shafts they sunk in the area and to generate electricity for the nearby bunkhouse. They found coal in every location they drilled, but later decided not to open a mine here. Originally, they planned to sell the coal to the east-west railroad that ran through Hinton and Jasper. By the time they were ready to develop the mine, a parallel railroad was built through Calgary and the northern railroad folded. The coal company didn't think it would be economical to haul coal from up here to Calgary so they never developed these mines.

"On one of my trips awhile back, I ran into an outfitter friend of mine and an old timer looking over the steam engine. I asked the old timer if he'd ever seen an engine like that. He said, 'I was the one who drove the mules that dragged that engine back in here in 1928, young feller. It was a terrible winter and I nearly froze to death before I got out of here'."

Dave also showed us a grave up on top of the hill. The Willmore map pointed out a dozen pioneer grave sites in Willmore, but it didn't mention this one. Jessica found a grouse feather for her dream catcher near the grave.

"There's that hawk again," Emily said, pointing up to a red-tailed hawk cruising over the valley. We had noticed it earlier in the day and it seemed to follow us as we moved east along the ridge. It flew so effortlessly, gliding on the thermals coming up from the sun-drenched valley.

As we rode to the end of the ridge, to the east we saw the Mountain Trail we had ridden in on the first day; in the valley below us, we saw the Indian Trail our pack train took to camp; the Thoreau Trail with the steam engine to the north and Eagle's Nest Pass Trail to the south. All the trails spread out below us like a giant map.

The trail down the hill to the valley turned out to be steep, twisty and tricky with tree branches reaching out to snag me at every turn. Emily and Jessica did a magnificent job of riding, staying out of trouble and never complaining. We finally made it to the camp about 7 p.m., just in time for supper.

Supper consisted of salmon casserole, corn, baked potato and fruit salad for dessert. Eight or ten of us sat at the supper table a long time swapping stories of our adventures of the day. The hikers, riders and wranglers had each covered different ground that day and each had tales of beautiful flowers, interesting wildlife or ornery mules to relate. Then Florence took some close-up, glamour photos of Emily and Jessica.

"Looks like they have lit another fire on Rock Creek," Dave C said pointing to the black smoke billowing up to the south of camp. "The black smoke indicates a hot fire," Dave explained. "White smoke comes from a cool fire that is burning itself out." Sure enough, in a few minutes the smoke changed from black to white and within 15 minutes died out. Several helicopters buzzed over the camp heading for Rock Creek.

"There's someone hanging from the helicopter," Emily yelled as it flew over dangling something underneath. I took the binoculars and saw a water bucket hanging from a cable below the helicopter.

"They fly over a lake, come down low and fill the water bucket and then fly to the fire and drop the water on it," Dave C explained.

Florence took a glamour-shot close-up of Emily

After dark Emily came running up to the campfire and yelled, "There's an animal in the corral."

I took a flashlight and walked to the corral with her. I pointed the flashlight to where she saw the animal and the eyes of a large hare shone like taillights. It hopped out of the corral, sat a minute and then hopped back in apparently to eat some of the oats the horses spilled on the ground. The hare sat there eating oats

And Jessica

while Emily and Jessica walked up to within five feet of it. As they stood there, the hare hopped away and then hopped back and ate some more. Our last camp had a pet deer and this camp had a pet hare.

Chapter 18

Riding Back to the Trail Head

Another gorgeous golden sunrise with the bluest sky I've ever seen. Dave M said one reason the sky looked so blue in the mountains was that the mountains limited your view of the horizon. The higher up you looked, the bluer the sky appeares because you were looking through less atmosphere. Without the mountains, you could look all the way down to the horizon and through a hundred miles of dirty atmosphere. Because of the high mountains, you were only looking through a few miles of atmosphere. I still think the sky was just naturally bluer in Canada than it is in the United States.

Marilyn and Anna served us a hearty breakfast of corn-beef hash, eggs and biscuits---a working man's meal. Emily went back for a second egg.

The staff got up early and had the horses in before 6 a.m. They started saddling the horses right after breakfast.

Emily, Jessica and I read another chapter about Kaya and her horse after breakfast and I tape-recorded the girls relating some of the highlights of the trip. After the taping session, they ran down to the creek to play while the wranglers packed the horses. There's something magical about a fast-flowing stream to children of all ages. The hikers left camp about 9 a.m. and the rest of us rode out about noon.

While passing through the lower Eagle's Nest Camp, Anna pointed out a pure white monkshood flower among the normal bluish–purple flowers.

"I've never seen an albino monkshood before," Anna said.

"I've never even heard of albino flowers," I replied. "It sure is pretty."

Anna, Andy and I rode at the front of the pack train while Emily and Jessica brought up the rear with Wendy and Marilyn.

The smoke from the forest fire blotted out the sun

The horses behaved very well today, staying in line and not bucking their packs off or fighting. At several points in the straight trail, I could look back and see all the horses strung out in a line—an amazing sight.

About halfway to the trail head, the sky turned bluish-gray with smoke; the sun faded to a dull orange. The smoke-filtered sun turned everything a strange shade of orange—the horses, the people, the rocks and the trees. It looked like a Star Wars' movie landscape. The Rock Creek fire burned less than six miles away, just one mountain ridge between us. The smell of acrid smoke filled the air.

We caught up with our four hikers at one of the Wild Hay River crossings. They had donned their rubber-soled sandals to wade the river and sat soaking their feet in the sparkling water on the far side before putting their hiking boots back on.

"Can we dunk Emily and Jessica in the horse water trough when we get to the trail head?" Wendy asked out of earshot of the

Lookout Point provided a commanding view of Rock Lake and the valley

twins. "The weather's nice and warm and I'll make some excuse to have them take their boots off before we dunk them."

"Sure," I agreed, wondering if I might get dunked too.

By not stopping for lunch, we made good time, nearing the trail head about 3 p.m. Dave M, Emily, Jessica and I turned off at the Green Gate to ride up to Lookout Point while the wranglers took the horses to the trail head.

Lookout Point is on a bluff about 600 feet above Rock Lake. The point offered a commanding view of the 20-mile-long valley where Rock Creek drained into Rock Lake. It also offered an excellent view of the snow-covered mountain ranges in all directions. I'm sure Indians and explorers climbed up to this very spot to get a view of this rugged country before they tried to cross the mountain ranges.

As we rode down from Lookout Point, Anna stepped out of the woods onto the trail holding sprigs of twinflowers. Two pale pink bell-shaped twinflowers grew on the long stems of this ground-covering shrub. Anna handed them to the twins and me.

"I've been looking for these the entire trip and found them riding into the trail head," Anna said. "I thought the twins should put them in their dried flower collection." (See their dried flower collection on page 78.)

"Thanks, Anna," the girls said.

As we rode into the trail head I expected Wendy and Dave Carnell to come over and get the twins for the water trough dunking.

"The water trough is dry," Wendy said when I rode Dancer into the corral. "Nobody filled it since we left two weeks ago."

We tied up our horses, emptied the saddlebags and started sorting through the pack boxes looking for our belongings. As I found a bag, I carried it over to the car and loaded it. After 30 minutes of searching through the boxes, I located all of our gear. Emily and Jessica said good-bye to Pepper and Yeller, and got hugs from all of the hikers and wranglers.

"The trip turned out better than I ever expected," I told Dave Manzer as we shook hands. "You and the staff delivered on all counts—adventure, beauty, comfort, food, entertainment and fellowship. One of the things that impressed me about your outfit was how supportive all the wranglers were to each other. I never heard one of the staff argue about whose turn it was to shovel horse manure out of the corral, wash dishes or bring the firewood in. Everyone pitched in and did whatever needed to be done. You've got an exceptional bunch of people working with you."

"You're right, they're top-notch. We sure enjoyed having you along," Dave said. "The twins are great horsewomen and great campers. I can't remember when we've had less trouble and more fun with children on a ride."

We hopped in our car and waved good-bye as we drove out of the parking lot.

"You watch for animals on the left side, I'll watch on the right side and grandpa can watch ahead," Emily suggested as we drove through the forest.

"There's a bear!" Jessica yelled a few minutes later. "Stop grandpa."

I stopped the car next to a meadow. About 100 feet away, where the meadow met the forest, a young black bear looked up from eating berries and stared at us. I got out of the car and took a couple of photos as he went back to eating berries. I'd estimate the bear stood about three–feet tall and weighed between 100 and 200 pounds. We watched several minutes while the bear foraged for berries and then we drove off, leaving him to finish his meal in peace.

"Let's stop at the Dairy Queen," Jessica suggested.

We stopped and I called my daughter to let her know we'd completed the horseback ride safely.

"We got lost," Emily told her mother first thing. "I wasn't sure I'd ever see you again."

"Grandpa grew a beard," Jessica said as her big news item of the day.

"We'll be home about supper time tomorrow," I told Judy.

Since the Hinton Dairy Queen still didn't have chocolate ice cream, Emily ordered a Dilly Bar and Jessica a hot-fudge sundae.

As the clerk handed me our order, Dave Manzer, Florence, Ray and Hannah came in to Dairy Queen. More hugs all around.

"Haven't seen you in an hour," Dave said as he ordered a hot dog.

"We saw a bear," Jessica announced excitedly and then she and Emily gave Dave a detailed report.

We finished our ice cream, said good-bye again and headed for Edmonton. It started raining a little ways out of Hinton and rained harder and harder until I couldn't see 50 feet down the highway. I slowed down to 25 mph and fought against the gusty winds to keep the car on the road. The weather report came on as soon as I turned on the radio.

"A tornado has been sighted near Wildwood, Alberta," the CBC-One radio announcer said. "Torrential rains and winds gusting up to 100 kilometers an hour are reported."

"Where are we, grandpa?" Emily asked.

"We just passed through Wildwood, Alberta."

The rain slacked off enough that I could resume highway speed and the winds died down as we proceeded down Highway 16. A bright rainbow appeared as the sky cleared behind us and the sun peeked through. A few minutes later the rainbow turned into a double rainbow. It seems that every time I take the twins on an adventure we see twin rainbows. As the sun sunk lower in the sky, the end of the rainbow appeared to move closer and closer.

"The end of the rainbow is just on the other side of the highway," I said. "Maybe we should stop and look for the pot of gold."

"You can't get to the end of the rainbow, grandpa," Emily said. "My science teacher told me it keeps moving as you try to catch up with it." Another myth exposed.

We drove into the Downtown Edmonton Best Western Motel about 9 p.m. I stayed at this motel in 1999 when I bicycled from Ohio to Alaska. Right after registering, we changed into our swimsuits and headed for the pool. The pool felt cool, not as cold as the mountain lake, but cool. Emily, Jessica and I alternated between the main pool and the delightfully warm hot tub.

About 9:30 p.m. a thunderstorm passed through with bright flashes of lightning that lit up the parking lot like daylight.

"Do we have to get out of the pool?" Jessica asked.

"No, I don't think so," I said. "We should be okay unless the lightning hits the building and even then, we're probably just as safe in the water as sitting in a chair on the wet floor."

We swam until the pool closed and then I went to the front desk to ask about the guest laundry.

"Yes, it's down the hall, but it's only open from 8 a.m. to 8 p.m.," the desk clerk said. "The noise bothers the people in the adjacent rooms."

That didn't help us, we would be on our way to the airport by 8 a.m. Jessica's sweater and my blue jeans needed washings. While Emily and Jessica watched TV, I washed the sweater and jeans in the bathtub, Italian style, stomping on them like grapes. I wrung them out, soaked up the excessive water with a towel and hung them up to dry.

"Bedtime," I said at midnight.

"Where's my kitty Boots?" Emily asked.

"Where did you have it last?" I asked.

"In my bed this morning," Emily replied. I checked her sleeping bag and couldn't find it.

"Maybe it ended up in the staff sleeping bag we used." (In fact that's what happened. Boots flew home via airmail a week later.)

Chapter 19

Get Me to the Plane on Time

Wrrrrrrrrrrrrrrrrrrrr the hair drier roared as I dried Jessica's sweater at 5 a.m. It took 30 minutes to get her sweater dry enough to wear. Then I started on my blue jeans. Drying a pair of Levi jeans with a hand-held hair dryer is not the fastest way to do it, but I didn't have access to a clothes dryer. It took an hour and a half to dry them including two five-minute cool-down periods when the hair dryer overheated and kicked off.

Emily and Jessica woke up at 7 o'clock, dressed and we checked out of the motel. I found Smitty's Pancake House nearby and we ordered breakfast: Fruit Loops for Jessica; pancakes for Emily and the full monty for me; bacon, eggs and pancakes.

After breakfast, I commented that we had a little over two hours before our flight left. No hurry, we had plenty of time. I thought. The North Saskatchewan River cuts Edmonton in half and the north/south streets in the top half of the town don't line up with the streets below the river. Instead of driving down the street, across the bridge and straight on to the airport, I had to jog right to get onto the bridge, cross the river, drive west and then intercept 104th Street south to the airport. I made it across the High Level Bridge okay, but got into the wrong lane while I drove west and ended up heading north and crossing back over the river on the Walterdale Hill Bridge.

Okay, don't panic. Turn left and get back over to the original bridge and try it again, I thought. I turned left at my first opportunity, River Valley Road, and started looking for the exit to the High Level Bridge. As I passed under the bridge, I realized I couldn't get to the High Level Bridge from River Valley Road. No sweat, I'll take the next bridge. Five minutes later I exited, turned south and crossed the river again. According to the crude map in the Edmonton guidebook, I could follow that road to 82nd and follow it west to intercept 104th, which would take us to the airport. I drove and drove and we were still only down to the 90s. Finally I came to 82nd, stopped, looked at the map and realized I was at the intersection of 82nd Street and 82nd Avenue. Dummkopf! I had been on 82nd Avenue for the past 15 minutes. Why does Edmonton use numbers for both the east-west avenues and the north-south streets?

I turned around and headed back up 82nd Avenue looking for 104th Street. We now had a little over an hour until plane time. For international flights, the airlines advised me to arrive at the check-in two hours early because of all the new security procedures. I looked in the rearview mirror and didn't see any police cars, nor any in front so I pushed my speed up a little above the 50 kilometers/ hour (km/h) legal limit and flew back up 82nd Avenue. Unbeknownst to me, Edmonton had radar cameras and the camera at 82nd Avenue and 96th Street snapped a beautiful color photo of me going 67 km/ h. (A month later I received a very nice letter from the Edmonton Police Service advising me of my offense and the $110 fine.) We made it back to 104th Street and I headed south to the airport, arriving with less than an hour before the scheduled flight time. I still had to drop off the car, transport six bags weighing 150 pounds to the airline check-in counter, get our tickets, wait in line to go through security, carry our bags to immigration, get our passports stamped and get to the gate.

As we ran past the rental car counter, I threw the rental contract and keys to the pretty Thrifty agent and raced across the street to the airline check-in with Emily and Jessica dragging their stuffed animals and backpacks. Fortunately, there was a short line at the Northwest Airlines ticket counter.

"Good morning, Mr. Johnson," said the ticket agent. "Did you have a nice vacation in Canada?"

"Yes, we did," I said still gasping for breath from our quarter-mile dash.

"Here are your tickets and seat assignments. Thanks for flying Northwest."

We carried our bags to immigration, got them pre-cleared and sent them off to the baggage conveyor belt. As we went though passport control I had to produce Judy's letter authorizing me to travel with my granddaughters. Then I got stopped at security and had to remove my shoes and belt. As Jessica passed her backpack through the x-ray, the agent stopped the belt and called her over.

"What do you have in the bag?" she asked Jessica.

"My toys, stuffed animals and fossil collection," Jessica replied.

"Can we look in the bag?"

"Yes."

The agent dumped the contents of Jessica's backpack on the counter, sifted through her stuff and lifted up a four-inch long rock. "What's this?" the agent asked.

"That's a heart-shaped rock I found up in the mountains," Jessica replied. "I'm taking it home to my mama."

The rock had a perfect heart shape, rounding to a "V" at the top and a point at the bottom. The agent called several of her colleagues over to see the pretty rock, then put it back in Jessica's backpack along with the other contents.

"Thank you," she said. "That's a beautiful rock. I'm sure your mother will be impressed."

We hurried to the gate and arrived just a few minutes before they boarded. I would never have heard the end of it if we missed our flight and had to stay in Edmonton another day. Emily and Jessica had just enough time to buy a couple of Beanie Babies and use up the rest of my Canadian money.

During the flight I tape-recorded some more of Emily and Jessica's comments on the highlights of their horseback trip.

"I thought the people were nice," Jessica said. "They did fun things with us and no one yelled at us."

"I liked the horses," Emily added. "I think I'm going to work with horses when I grow up."

"I remember when we crossed the river and got in these really, really tall willows," Jessica said. "And there was a snare in the willows that catches animals. Dave got his foot caught in it and it almost jerked him off the saddle. Then I was looking around and I saw a black bear—it died because it got caught in another snare with its arm hanging up. It didn't look like it had been there long because the bugs hadn't got in him yet. Grandpa took a picture of the bear. I didn't understand why they put the snares up there in the first place."

"The trappers put them there to catch animals like wolves or lynx."

"But how does the wolf know he's supposed to get in it and not the bear?" Jessica asked.

"Obviously they don't know," I agreed.

"I was scared when we got lost in the woods," Emily said. "I didn't think I'd ever see my mommy again. I thought we would have to sleep in the woods and make a pillow out of the grass. Then I saw Anna waving to us and I was happy."

"I liked it when we climbed that really steep mountain," Jessica said. "The wind came up and it was blowing really, really, really hard. I had to crawl on the ground to keep from being blown away. We went up where the sheep were and it was real rocky. Then we slid down this big hill on the loose rocks and I got rocks in my boots. It took a long time to get down because it was so far. When we stopped, we saw seven sheep. Then we found geodes with pretty crystals inside. Hannah showed us the dinosaur bones in the wall. It was a little baby dinosaur about a foot long."

"I liked it when we went swimming in the lake with Wendy," Emily said. "The water was a little bit cold. I stopped when the water came up to my legs. Jessica went until she got up to her tummy. Wendy went almost all the way and got up to her neck."

"What were you wearing?" I asked.

"Nothing," Emily replied, "just my birthday suit. Wendy was wearing her birthday suit too. It was fun because no boys were allowed."

"I remember when we rode up in the mountains and our horses fell through the snow." Jessica said. "I wasn't scared because it was really, really fun. Some of the snow up there was pink because of the allergies (algae). Wendy called it watermelon snow. And when we got through the snow, we saw some elk (caribou)."

"I liked it when Jessica lost her hat on the horse and Avery picked up the hat and gave it to Wendy," Emily said.

"My horse's name was Yeller, but Wendy called it Mustard," Jessica said.

"That's because Old Yeller was the name of a dog in a movie," I explained. "The dog died and it made Wendy sad to think about Old Yeller so she calls him Mustard."

"I remember when I was riding Eeyore through the woods and he ran right through the trees," Emily said. "I thought the branches were going to hit me so I ducked backwards and lay down on Eeyore's back. After we got back on the trail, Hannah took Eeyore's rope and led him. It was funny because Eeyore's lead rope kept getting stuck under Victor's (Hannah's horse's) tail as we went up the hill."

"One day we rode up to a mountain (Blue Grouse Pass) where we could climb," Emily said. "Grandpa and I climbed up the mountain and we saw 20 goats. The wind was blowing really hard and I fell down in the grass a couple of times. When we got to the snow I slid down. It was really fun."

"I found a lot of fossils one day when we hiked up by the sheep," Jessica said. "One of them was a foot long, but grandpa wouldn't carry it home for me."

"Anna carried me across the stream by the fossils because she didn't want me to get my shoes wet," Emily said. "And Hannah carried Jessica."

169

"The wild animals impressed me," I said. "I never expected
to see so many animals:

        4 grizzly bears
        2 black bears
        1 moose
        48 elk
        9 caribou
        3 mule deer
        50 big horn sheep
        and 22 mountain goats."

"You girls also impressed me. You spent 16 days in the saddle and never complained or whined. That's pretty impressive for a couple of nine year olds who never spent more than an hour a week on a horse before."

The flight home went smoothly with a quick change of planes in Minneapolis. In Cincinnati, the baggage claim lady informed us that Emily's suitcase went to Miami, Florida, on vacation and wouldn't be back for a few days. All the rest of the bags arrived safely. On the drive home, we stopped at Taco Bell because it had been three weeks since the twins had a fast-food fix.

"Mama," Emily said excitedly as she hugged her mother, "we saw bears and got lost and learned to shoot a slingshot!"

"We got to trot and Wendy taught me how to spin a rope," Jessica said as she wrapped her arms around her mother's waist.

"I missed you both," Judy said with tears in her eyes. "I'm glad you're home safe and sound."

APPENDIX A
Take-to Willmore List

Allen's List

<u>Clothes</u>
3- pair Levis
2- short sleeve shirts
4 long sleeve shirt
2 polo shirts
7-underwear
7-undershirts
7 pair socks
2 T-shirts
swim suit
towel
2-wash clothes
running shorts
sun hat
pull-over hat
wool gloves
hooded windbreaker
Gortex pants
Gortex jacket
Sweat shirt
4-pair wool socks
long underwear
6 hankies
walking shoes
hiking boots

<u>Horse Stuff</u>
Reef shoes

Biking gloves
Rain poncho
Dry-bag
digital camera
camera batteries
analog camera
10-slide film 35mm
camera batteries
duct tape
wire
Cord
Rope
Compass
Maps
Waterproof matches
First aid kit
3-Flashlights
Batteries
Knife
Leatherman tool
Whistle
Signal mirror
plastic bags
ziploc bags
water bottle
field glasses
Accessories
Airline tickets

171

Passports
Judy's approval letter
Computer
Disks
Telephone plug
Power plug adapter
Tape recorder
Tapes
batteries
Phone numbers
Address book
e-mail addresses
magnifying glass
backpack & sports bag

Games
Uno
Dominos
Cards
Paper & Markers
Books
pens

Toiletries
Overnight kit
Aspirin
Neosporin
Sunscreen
Children's aspirin
Cough medicine
Cold medicine

Alka Seltzer
10 packs of Tide detergent

Emily's & Jessica's List
Boots
Reef shoes
Sneakers or regular shoes
4-Wool socks
7-regular socks
7-underwear
4-short-sleeve-shirts
long underwear
4-jeans or long pants
2-pair short pants
4 long-sleeve shirts
2-sweat shirts
1 pair waterproof pants
Hooded windbreaker
Wool hat & Sun hat
Night gown
Biking gloves
Wool gloves
Blankie
1-Beanie baby
Journal
Camera
Water bottle
Sunglasses
Whistle
Back pack
Tooth-brush

APPENDIX B
What Did it Cost

Willmore Adventure	$7,767 (in U.S. dollars, 3 people)
Air fares	1,259 (3 people)
Rental car	450
Hotel	100 (1 night)
Maps	145
Camp clothes	250
Film & developing	100
Airport parking	<u>108</u>
Total	**$10,034**

APPENDIX C
Horses

Name	Breed	Attributes
Abelard	Morgan/Qtr Horse/Arab	Six-year-old, pinto colored. Is a trained driving horse and is training to do circus tricks with Avery, Wendy and Heloise.
Auzzie	Australian Std. Breed-20 year	Race horse – tattoo on leg. Raced for 8 years on track.
Big Guy		One of the oldest horses at 26. Steady as a rock. Jumped over a bear in the willows years ago with Dave M riding him.
Billy	Eight years	Seems to be around when bad things happen. Broke Joshes ribs. Goes crazy when pack train nears home.
Black Heart	Quarterhorse Probably Eight years	Lazy, obnoxious. Tosses his head. Andy loves him. He's willing and enjoys working in the pack train. Very strong, but requires a strong rider.
Black Jack	Mule Eight years	young and aggressive, wants to be at the head of the pack. Once he gets there he is very helpful in keeping the other horses in line behind. Loves to roll in the dust when he has his pack on. Wendy's favorite mule.
Blaze	Palomino Four years	Very responsive. When you ask him to do something, he doesn't ask why? Dave M has been riding him for the past two years so he is learning to be a great,

		unflappable lead horse.
Blue	18 years	Blind in left eye. Dependable; will go forever; always ready to get you out of trouble. Very willing. Has a great lope and will lope for hours. A bit of a handful for a light-handed rider.
Buckwheat	mule Six years	Dependable. The most alert animal in the outfit. Got into trouble during summer 2003. Lost his load twice and ran over Wendy and Phillipa in August.
Bug	mule – 9 yrs	Cute as a bug
Dancer	Appaloosa 9-10 years	Well trained. Spent some years in Dressage training side steps as in "side pass." Very good for a saddle horse. Likes to jump. Flexible. A well-trained rider can make this horse do many things without visible contact, but someone who hasn't had a lot of instructions might not know they were giving the horse a command and Dancer would execute it. Won "Best all around horse" award in 2003.
Eeyore	Fjord 21 years old	Fearless in his youth, but has settled down to be most dependable horse in the lot. Dave C's favorite because Eeyore concentrates and pulls so hard when he's hauling in wood. He won't give up on the heaviest log so it's up to us to

		make sure we don't give him too big a load.
Ernie	Tennessee Walking horse 16 years old	On loan from Deb Muldoon. Not a horse to share with guests. Loves to go! Fastest horse at a walk in the herd. Thinks he's in charge when working the pack train. Keeps eye on everyone front and back. Will bite Eeyore for walking too slow.
Festus	mule 10 years old	Strong willed, likes to buck load off. Nice once you get to know him. Don't give him sweets or he'll search all you pockets for more.
Heloise	Morgan/Qtr Horse/Arab	Five year old, pinto colored. Is a trained driving horse and is training to do circus tricks with Avery, Wendy and brother Abelard.
Jack	Line-back dun 25-years old	Real trooper. Until he was 15, he was a bronk, but got over it. Dave M rode him for 13 years.
Jack Mule	mule Old	Always wants to be with Jill. Brother and sister
Jill	mule Old	Broken to drive. She and Jack are the two most dependable mules anywhere.
Jay Jay	Chestnut Old	Old pack horse. Only horse in the herd that consistently unties himself. Came from the Okanagan.
Jane	Fiord	quiet, nicest one to handle

Lefty	Packhorse	Likes to be in front of pack. Dependable. Number one pack horse.
Little Man	Chestnut/ Arabian 7-years old	Hannah's choice. Very smart and willing. Previously pack horse, but promoted to riding horse this year. Can open electric fence gates by gripping the gate handle with his teeth and unhooking it..
Midnight	Arabian 8 years old	A little rusty as a riding horse. Has been hanging out with Little Man in the pack string for last few years, but ridden part of 2003. With some more experience will be a great saddle horse.
Pepper	Appaloosa 18 years old	Nice, wants to be with Yeller, good for guests. Pepper and Yeller have a habit of not coming in from pasture each morning with the rest of the herd and of being the furthest away, sometime many miles. Yeller remembers where all the best grass grows so Yeller and Pepper are generally the fattest at the end of the year. Dave got them from outfitter Gord Utry in Durwell when he sold out.
Poncho Villa	10 years old	Bossy, orders other horses around. Kicked three horses. A good ride if you let him know you're the boss right

Randy	Quarterhorse Paint Maybe 10	away. Dependable and well trained. Was a show horse in his other life.
Redwood	Australian Std. Breed	Bought him off the track many years ago. 20 years old
Sally	Fjord	Eager. Jumps nicely. Doesn't let being short stop her from going where everyone else goes.
Skeeter	gray jenny Mule-10 yrs	Skittish. She'll lay down and roll over for a pail of oats
Silver	Mare	Anna's horse. A sweetheart. Has had lots of paint colts and fillies and is a good mom. Dependable, except when left to her own devices. It is not accident that most of the herd are geldings. They are less trouble.
Smudge	Arabian 22 years	Dressage trained; lopes slowly. Not a horse for guests because if he gets excited there is almost no stopping him.
Victor	Fjord	Hyper, responsive, bucks. Likes caramel candy.
Yeller	Palomino 19 years	dependable, good for guests. Great lead horse. Knows all the trail and where all the camps are. You could get on

| | | him and he would take you there. |
| Willy | bay mule
8 years old | Riding mule in training. He's so big that we need to convince him that whatever it is we want him to do, he wants to do it too. Right now he won't do that. Largest member of the Wild Rose herd. |

Dave Manzer's mule philosophy: "If you have a bad mule that lives to be 40 years old, that's not a good deal!"

Alpine coltsfoot
Arnica
Beard-tongue
Beargrass
Bluebell
Bog orchid
Buttercup
Cinquefoil
Clover (purple)
Columbine (red, yellow,
    orange)
Cotton grass
Daisy fleabane
False Dandelion
False Hellebore
Forget-me-not
Gentian
Globeflower
Heather (pink, white)
Hedysarum
Horsetail
Labrador tea
Larkspur
Lupine (blue, pink)
Marsh marigold
Monkshood
Moss campion
Mountain Aven
Mountain daisy
Mountain fleabane
Paintbrush (red, yellow)

Riverbeauty
Silky Phacelia
Twinflower
Western Anemone
Western Clematis
White Camas
Wild rose
Wild white geranium
Woolly Lousewort
Yarrow

REFERENCES

Bush, Wendy, <u>Ascent of Dog – Working Dogs in the West;</u> Detselig Enterprises; Calgary, AB Canada 1998.
        ISBN 1-55059-174-6

Gadd, Ben, <u>Handbook of the Canadian Rockies</u>, Corax Press; Jasper, AB Canada, 1995.
        ISBN 0-9692631-1-2

Gardiner, John R., <u>Stone Fox</u>; Harper trophy; NY, NY; 1980.
        ISBN 0-690-03983-2

Shaw, Janet, <u>Changes for Kaya</u>; Pleasant Company; Middletown WI; 2002.
        ISBN 1-58485-434-0

Twain, Mark, <u>Innocents Abroad</u>; Harper and Brothers; NY, NY; 1869

INDEX

[ ]   **Willmore Horseback Adventure**

A 500-pound grizzly bear chased a ground squirrel a scant 100 feet from us while her twin cubs watched. Emily and Jessica sat quiet as church mice as the chase continues. With a flying leap, the sow bear caught the squirrel and fed it to her hungry cubs.

My 9-year-old twin granddaughters, Emily and Jessica, joined four hikers seven wranglers and me on 16-day horseback adventure in the Canadian Rocky Mountains of Alberta Canada. The Wild Rose Outfitters used 24 pack horsed and 10 riding horses to take us deep into the 1,700 square mile wilderness park without roads, bridges, houses or permanent residents.

We camped at six remote sites high in the Rocky Mountains. A sugar-coating of frost covered our tents each morning. During the day, we rode over snow-covered mountain passes, through virgin spruce forests, across rain-swollen rivers and along knife-edge ridges to see some of the most spectacular wilderness country in the world.

Our cook prepared gourmet meals in a wilderness camp environment: charcoal-grilled steak, pork chops, lasagna, shepard's pie and salmon with a different type of fresh salad every night and our choice of red and white wine for supper.

When Emily and Jessica weren't on the trail they were wading in the creek, chasing butterflies, shooting at tin cans with their slingshots, fishing, roasting marshmallows, reading stories, making dream catchers, looking for fossils or begging Dave to play the "Pickle" song on his guitar so they could sing along.

The horseback ride turned out to be the adventure of a lifetime.

ISBN 1-880675-08-0   **$15.00**

[ ] Kayaking Around Iceland

Emily and Jessica, the author's 8-year-old granddaughters, embarked on a kayaking trip in the Arctic Ocean around Iceland with the author and a friend. One of the days, the sunny, windless, glassy-smooth fjord turn into a gray, foamy torrent of wind-whipped white-capped waves in less than an hour. Paddling back to the mainland became an exciting adventure. The other days of kayaking turned out to be much more mundane. They experienced beautiful sunny, calm weather, picturesque green fjords, sparkling waterfalls, colorful puffin birds and snow-covered mountains in the background.

Besides kayaking, they visited waterfalls, geysers, glaciers, bird cliffs, geothermal pools and gorgeous black-sand beaches. Emily counted 1,004 waterfalls while they drove 2,000 miles through the Iceland countryside. One windy day they visited the Latrabjarg bird cliffs where millions of puffins, kittiwakes, gulls, and cormorants nest.   **ISBN 1-880675-07-2**   **$15.00**

[ ] ROLLERBLADING ACROSS HOLLAND

In the summer of 1998, Allen, Kelsey (11-years old) and Karla Reichert, a family friend, rollerbladed 365 miles around Holland carrying a backpack. They started in Amsterdam, skated to the coast of the North Sea, followed the coastline down to Belgium, skated in to Antwerp and back up to Amsterdam. They encountered windmills, dikes, polders, dams, canals, monasteries, medieval churches, a diamond factory, castles and beaches.

The trio averaged 25-miles per day by skating 5 to 7 hours. They stopped often to explore windmills, swim in the North Sea, tour the unique storm surge barriers that keeps the sea out of the Dutch lowlands, visit with the local people and see the local sights.

The food in Holland and Belgium was both delicious and attractively presented. They dined on lobster salads, chicken breast covered with nuts, Argentine steaks, Chinese and Japanese delicacies, a dozen kinds of pasta, and dozens of different cheeses

The trio agreed rollerbladed swam in the North Sea 10 times, ate 103 scoops of delicious Dutch ice cream, sampled 38 different kinds of cheese and attended a flower auction where 17-million flowers are sold each day. I'd call that a successful trip! **$15.00**

ISBN 1-880675-04-8

[ ]   BIKING TO THE ARCTIC CIRCLE

"Bike to the Arctic Circle? Impossible! There's ice and snow up there," my friend said. Regardless, I did cycle to the Arctic Circle.

As a child I dreamed of traveling the Alaskan Highway. When I started planning the trip our grandson agreed to bike the 1,000 mile Alaskan Highway portion. My office-mate rode the first 800 miles, our niece cycled across Canada and my neighbor rode the Alaskan portion.

The prettiest part of our lower-48-state ride was biking along the Mississippi River's Great River Road from Savanna IL to Minneapolis MN. Bald eagles soaring overhead, deer peeking out of the wooded hills and tugboats pushing barges up river.

Karen joined me in Regina SK and rode one week. We fought head winds across Sask., pedaling 14 hours one day to go 85 miles. The next day we covered the same distance in 6 hours with a tail wind.

Grandson Paul joined me in Edmonton AB. A few days later we biked into Dawson Creek, BC where the Alaskan Highway starts. Along the Alaskan Highway we encountered moose, deer, caribou, elk, buffalo, mountain sheep, wolves, black bear, grizzly bears, fox, lynx, coyotes, beaver, hares, porcupines, weasels, swans, eagles and owls.

At Whitehorse, Yukon Karla joined me and biked the final leg of the trip. In Fairbanks I switched to a mountain bike for the 200-miles of gravel road to the Arctic Circle. We spent the next night in Joy AK with the Carlsons who raised 23 children in a log cabin with no electricity, running water or indoor toilet.

On 24 June 1999 I biked across the Arctic Circle line, completing the 4,081-mile ride in 51days. Worth the effort? You bet!   **$15.00**

ISBN 1-880675-03-X

[ ] AUSTRALIA FROM THE BACK OF A CAMEL

The 12 camels plodded through Rainbow Valley in the Australian outback. Kelsey, the author's 7-year-old granddaughter, nudged her 1,000-pound camel in the belly and Charcoal charged off in a cloud of dust, galloping to the head of the line. The author and 3 of his grandchildren were on a 7-day camel safari in the middle of the Australian desert. They spent 8 hours a day riding camels in search of caves with Aboriginal paintings, fossils, desert animals and unusual flora and fauna. At night, the Johnsons slept on the ground around a huge fire to ward of the near-freezing temperature. It was winter in the desert, with daytime temperatures of 80 to 90F, but at night it dropped to 30 degrees F. They encountered wallabies, kangaroos, wedge-tailed eagles, dingos, emus and a variety of desert birds, lizards, snakes and spiders. The Johnsons sampled the desert foods, including eating a three-inch long witchery grub. The best part of the trip: "Running the camels across the dry lake-bed," Kelsey said. "Seeing how my grandchildren handled new situations," was Allen's reply.   **$16.95**

ISBN 1-880675-02-1

[ ]   BIKING ACROSS THE DEVIL'S BACKBONE

A 9-year-old and her grandfather pedaled 600 miles across the mid-West in search of adventure. Enroute they explored Cave-in-Rock on the Ohio River, the Garden of the Gods in southern Illinois, visited an ostrich farm in Mt. Vernon, spent the night with the monks at St. Meinrad Monastery, toured Lincoln's boyhood home in southern Indiana and pedaled over the razorback Devil's Backbone. Tracy maintained her good humor and high spirits while pedaling up to 65 miles a day through the hilly route in 95-degree heat. The best part of the trip? "The day at the monastery," replied Tracy. "Spending time with my granddaughter," explained Allen.   **$15.95**

ISBN 1-880675-01-3

[ ]   CANOEING THE WABASH

An adventure-packed 500-mile long trip canoeing down the Wabash River with the author and his 10-year-old grandson. From Fort Recovery, Ohio, they dragged the canoe through the shallow, upper Wabash, fought raging rapids and survived a 14-hour long thunder-lightening storm. At night the pair camped and fished along the banks of the river. They encountered deer, raccoons, muskrats, rabbits, beaver, gars and pileated woodpeckers during their 16-day journey along the still-wild river. The trip was a physical challenge and an educational experience. Along the river they visited Ft. Recovery, Tippecanoe Battlegrounds and the George Rogers Clark monument. After paddling

189

one-quarter-million strokes they finally reached their destination—the Ohio River. The author weaves a tale of adventure, history and humor into a delightful package. **$13.95**

ISBN 1-880675-00-5

[ ]   DRIVE THROUGH RUSSIA? IMPOSSIBLE!

In 1981, the author and his wife rented a car and drove 4,000 miles through the Communist Soviet Union by themselves. This book describes the 3-week odyssey through the ancient countryside and modern bureaucracy. When the Johnsons first entered the Soviet Union, the officials informed them they would be staying the in the Pribaltiskaya Hotel that night in Leningrad. "What is the name of our hotel in Novgorod tomorrow night?" Allen asked. "It is not necessary for you to know. Tomorrow we will tell you where you will be staying." The author found that in the Soviet Union, information was power and the officials were very reluctant to give it away. With a basic understanding of the Russian language learned from 3 years of tutoring in Dayton before the trip, the Johnsons traveled from town to town, purchased food and gasoline, interpreted the meager road maps and visited with the Russian people. They found the people curious, kind and helpful. Travel with the Johnsons and enjoy a vivid picture of their daily discoveries, pleasures and frustrations.   **ISBN 0-553-06695-6**   **$10.95**

Order With This Convenient Coupon

Creative Enterprises
1040 Harvard Blvd.
Dayton OH 45406-5047

Please send me the books I have checked above. I am enclosing $____________ (please add $2.00 for postage/handling. Ohio residents add 6.5% tax). Send check or money order. You can also order from the Internet: **http://www.creative-enterprises.org, toll free from 888-BOOKS77, or E-mail allen45406@aol.com**

Name____

Address____

City_______________________________ State ـــــ Zip Code ________

Allow 2—4 weeks for delivery.